SPIRITUALITY AND BUSINESS: A CHRISTIAN VIEWPOINT

An open letter to Christian leaders in times of urgency

Philippe de Woot

Routledge
Taylor & Francis Group

LONDON AND NEW YORK

Originally published by Lethielleux-Desclée de Brouwer (Paris, 2009) with the title *Lettre ouverte aux décideurs chrétiens en temps d'urgence.*

First published in English in 2013 by GSE Research Ltd

Published 2017 by Routledge
2 Park Square, Milton Park, Abingdon, Oxon OX14 4RN
711 Third Avenue, New York, NY 10017, USA

Routledge is an imprint of the Taylor & Francis Group, an informa business

Copyright © Desclee de Brouwer, 2009

Typeset in India by OKS Prepress Services, Chennai, India.

ISBN: 978-1-909201-09-5 (pbk)

ACKNOWLEDGEMENTS

This essay is dedicated to leaders who dared to do things differently

Albert de Mun
Léon Bekaert
Edouard Leclercq
Robert Ouimet
Muhammad Yunus

And a few others...
My warmest thanks go to:

Ignace Berten, O.P., of ESPACES – Spiritualities, Cultures and Society in Europe

Paul Dembinski, of the Observatoire de la Finance in Geneva who agreed to read the manuscript and enhance it with their suggestions

Edouard Herr, S.J. Spiritual Advisor for the International Christian Union of Business Executive (UNIAPAC), who was kind enough to write the preface

TABLE OF CONTENTS

PREFACE

This book automatically hands us a comprehensive and radical viewpoint. Indeed, it undertakes to change the economic model and design of the company. This may seem like a lot all at once. But let us remember that at the beginning of his career, Ph. de Woot published a book that made history: *La doctrine de l'entreprise* (*The doctrine of the company*) (1968) and that throughout his research corporate social responsibility has been present in his thinking – we need only consult his recent publication: "Should Prometheus be bound? Corporate Global Responsibility" (2005) – and that ultimately he led the publication of a large interdisciplinary work on globalisation: *Les défis de la Globalisation, Babel ou Pentecôte* (*The Challenges of Globalisation, Babel or Pentecost*) (2001). Bearing this in mind, we must acknowledge that we find ourselves before an eminent expert who is to be taken very seriously. This is the culmination of a long career as a teacher, researcher and consultant dedicated to all of these issues.

The work of our author can certainly contribute to the overall thinking, but also to that of the Christian employers as well as the Social Teachings of the Church. One often dealt with the corporation by stressing that within it, it was necessary to respect the dignity of each person, above all that of the workforce. This is obviously true, but there still lacks a real understanding of the enterprise. In short one has swung between, on the one hand, the corporation as a society of capital and contracts and, on the other hand, the corporation as a society of people. It is both of these things at once and one may combine it by noting that in the corporation there is a formal connection between people, but through the mediation of things, the exchange.

But Ph. de Woot went further by presenting an understanding of the corporation according to its purpose: "in a global economy, the aim of the company is to ensure economic and technical progress in view of real human progress and of democratic debate regarding the type of society that we would like to build together". In other words, the legitimacy of the corporation comes to it from its product or its service which promote economic progress, but it receives its purpose and its direction according to its contribution to genuine human progress and not simply by the formal and accountable increase in GDP. With this outlook Ph. de Woot finds himself in good company since the winner of the Nobel Prize for economics, Amartya Sen, has also argued in favour of a rethinking of the notion of progress for a long time.

As such we are in the presence of the articulation of the economic model that must produce, with the help of policy, real human development, and a company which is responsible for economic progress. Hence it is not enough to maximise profit or to remunerate shareholders; rather the anthropological direction of the corporation comes from its contribution to sustainable development within its three main aspects: economic, social and environmental. It is a model of integration of economic progress: the economic aspect is structured around politics and culture and all three around anthropology and ethics. An interesting debate could begin here between Ph. de Woot and A. Comte-Sponville who in his recent book, *Le capitalisme est-il moral? (Capitalism: Is it moral?)* (Comte-Sponville, 2004), precisely proceeds in a conflicting manner by separating the different orders as economic and moral. But only the process as described by our author gives a satisfactory *meaning* to the company and to economic dealings and fully legitimises these. He begins by questioning the human relevance of the product or service (*what-for?*), he poses the question of production methods, notably their environmental impact (*how?*), and that of the target market (*why?*), in short, the act of doing business takes on all of its human consistency and participates in the future of Mankind. One can as a Christian extend this idea by noting that the economic activity is also called upon to contribute to the work of salvation in Jesus Christ; both from the point of view of creation and redemption, the economic work participates in the building of the Kingdom.

If the corporation that creates economic progress receives its meaning from its contribution to economic growth and from its promotion of sustainable development, it must also be said that the company bears its share of responsibility for the successes or failures of the economic system as a whole. Two stumbling blocks must be avoided here: a paternalist model which wishes to take control of everything by taking away responsibility from all other actors or declaring itself powerless by ignoring the fact that the corporation exerts a considerable impact on its social and natural environment and that it must accept that. All in all, the company depends on "the outside", but it exerts its own activity and it influences in return "the outside", and for that it is responsible according to its specificity.

Some doubt, however, the application of the concept of responsibility to the corporation. According to them, one may speak of the responsibility of the businessman, but not of the company, as a corporate entity. However, if one looks at the criminal aspect of the responsibility, one notices that the company is considered responsible, as we recall, for example, in the awful case of the Union Carbide disaster in Bhopal, India (1984). Analogically, from an ethical point of view, the company has genuine responsibility, even if individual persons are the bearers and actors. Others feel uncomfortable with the adjective "corporate" that one often associates with responsibility when talking about the company. It is true that corporate means first of all the relationship between management and workforce within the company, whereas the responsibility that one thinks of is much broader, because it covers many other relationships, notably with the State, the environment, etc. In this sense it may be more appropriate to speak of corporate "societal" responsibility thereby defined by the very different structures and relationships upon which the company exercises its actions and therefore its responsibility.

In short, the view to which Ph. de Woot invites us to share takes account of the numerous stakeholders of the company and not only the shareholders. Indeed, the company maintains responsible links with several categories of stakeholders including the State and the environment. A focus group belonging to UNIAPAC (International Christian Union of Business Executives) developed an operational matrix where one lists in a line, eight stakeholders, and in columns, the three different human requirements of these stakeholders in order to indicate in each of the 24 cases, what specific liability the company must exercise. ("The Profit of Values", 2008)

Regarding corporate responsibilities, Ph. de Woot, raises an important issue: should the response to these stakeholder requirements be left to the sole goodwill of the corporations, or should these private initiatives be facilitated by legal measures under the responsibility of States and certain international organisations? Our expert opts for a mixed approach and he is right to do so. Without the contribution of the companies themselves, the pure constraint will remain ineffective, but without a legal framework, the dynamic risks falling down rapidly.

Professor de Woot builds his argument entirely on a spiritual and ethical outburst. This is all at once its strength and its weakness. He calls upon all men and all women of good faith in order to take stock of the full meaning of the company in these decisive times and he commits us to grasping our corresponding responsibilities. The challenge is enormous, but in reality the fate of Mankind depends on it. Will we face up to it?

This book also recommends itself by virtue of the personal involvement of the author in the field of spirituality. Indeed, this is inspiring and enlightening in numerous respects for the occupation of the businessman, for example by talking about this role as a service.

Because of the extensive knowledge of the author, notably Greco-Roman, reading is not only highly informative but also very pleasant.

Edouard Herr S.J.
August 2009

INTRODUCTION

Many Christian business leaders display an approach based on human dignity. They will strive, as best they can, to implement humane policies reflecting the values of the Gospel. It is a crucial issue even if this will is often limited by enormous competitive pressures.

But criticism of the economic system that they lead is often weak, superficial or non-existent, while the social doctrine of the Church is much more precise in this area, at least on some points. It is as if these leaders limit their criticism and their moral commitment to the company alone without taking account of the economic model in the benefits and shortcomings to which they contribute so actively.

Yet a question arises with ever greater acuity: can one act ethically in a system that is not? Can one remain Christian by leading a development model that incessantly flouts the values of the Kingdom?

Does globalisation not broaden the responsibility of economic leaders well beyond their own organisation to extend to the model of development of which they are the driving force?

Should the explosion of the financial bubble and the ensuing havoc bring us to question the failings of an increasingly powerful economic system but which, at the global level, is completely decoupled from ethics and politics?

Our development model is starting to become unsustainable. The destruction of the planet, growing inequalities, the extravagance of certain behaviour, situations of injustice, exclusion and alienation – do they not themselves herald the ghosts that from time to time haunt the history of Mankind and make it deviate from the paths of civilization?

So should we not go back to the age-old wisdom; that which resisted time and made it through the centuries?

Do not ignore the conversation of the wise and always revisit their proverbs
(Ecclesiasticus 8:8)

Naturally, the Christian leaders seek enlightenment and foundations in their great tradition of wisdom and commitment. It is this that allows us *to interpret the signs of the times in light of the Faith*.[1]

In doing this, should we not become more prophetic?

In the Bible, the role of the prophet is basically one of ethics and it is an ethic of action.

First of all, the prophet does not confine himself to the short term. He looks beyond the present time and he bypasses the immediate to consider the long-term consequences of our mistakes, of our failings or of our infidelities. He is *forward-looking*.[2] Then he casts a critical eye on society, power and the system into which our actions fit. He denounces injustices, oppressions and alienations of all kinds. Finally, he recalls the moral law and the values that should enlighten and lead us. He has the courage to say "this is wrong" or "this is good". He chooses his side, which in general is that of the weak, the poor and the oppressed.

Is this not also where the specificity of the movements of Christian business leaders and executives is found? Should we not challenge society more about the sense of a competitive race that is becoming globalised, spirals out of control and today leads to an unprecedented systemic crisis? Should we not also strive to transform the system itself and to render it more consistent with the requirements of the Common Good and an "ethic of foresight"?

Does the belief in an automatic link between economic development and the general interests of a globalising world not now fall within naivety or blindness?

The social doctrine of the Church[3] is however clear on this point and the last encyclical of Benedict XVI, *Caritas in veritate*, highlights the ambiguities of globalisation with no other purpose than economic growth and the pursuit of profit. But the Christian business leaders[4] appear hesitant to radically criticise the defects and deviations of an economic model that deteriorates, pollutes, alienates, excludes... The

---

[1] Buttet, N., *Semaine de mission*, La Hulpe, 2008.

[2] Vogels, W., *Les prophètes (The Prophets)*, Lumen vitae, Novalis, 2008.

[3] Pontifical Council for Justice and Peace, *Compendium of the Social Doctrine of the Church*, Paris, Bayard, Cerf, Fleurus-Mame, 2008. See also Berten, I., et al. *Enterrée, la doctrine sociale? (Is social doctrine buried?)* Bruxelles, Lumen Vitae, 2009.

[4] See notably UNIAPAC's paper, *The Profit of Values*, 2008.

criticism bears on certain points but the system itself appears insufficiently challenged, as much in its global failures as in its excessive financialisation.

Similarly, it seems to me that these leaders have failed so far to lead with depth and to issue a reflection on their *specific* role and on the *purpose (the raison d'être)* of the company. The function of innovation, creativity and technical progress is rarely at the heart of the debate. And yet, it is at the very heart of the process of doing business. It is through this that man's economic development has happened since the dawn of time and there would be much to say on the role of *co-creators* of businessmen and of companies, on its nobility and its ambiguities. Too often, even in the encyclicals, the purpose of the company is reduced to the production and distribution of goods and services, while it is much more fundamental than that: it is the company which initiates and guides economic and technical progress.

Indeed, it is through innovation that the real competitive struggles play out in our market economy: *Creative destruction* is its primary mode of operation. This is far from being indifferent with regard to ethical and spiritual plans, notably in terms of the acceleration of technical progress, of its direction by the only solvent markets and of the increasingly rapid and exclusive seizure of scientific knowledge by economic actors.

The great human wisdoms have clearly understood the ambiguity of technical progress with no other purpose than itself and the need, under pain of curse, to guide it by and submit it to political and ethical choices. The significance of such choices appears in all civilisations. This is the theme of apocalyptic speeches, blessings and also great curses. It is also that of the comments on the law which protects raises and leads people to wisdom, harmony and development for all.

The dangers which threaten us do not cease to grow. The future of the planet and the survival of Mankind are in question while many of us continue to trust the current economic system when a radical evolution is necessary and urgent.

Do we not then resemble that man *who refused to believe they had set fire to his house because he had the key in his pocket? (Tocqueville)*

Companies themselves cannot do it alone but they can play a decisive role in it by becoming more responsible. But it will take a transformation much deeper than that imagined today by most economic actors. Should Christian leaders not be part of the vanguard of reformers that could transform the businesses and the system that they lead?

If the movement of corporate social responsibility consists of sticking new labels on old practices, it will not become a transforming force and will not be taken seriously. This movement will only succeed in influencing the evolution of our development model if it renews the very purpose of the company and its role in the construction of a collective global future.

A radical change in corporate culture is needed to help transform our economic system and to make it socially legitimate. It is not concerned with destroying or replacing it but with humanising and directing it further towards the Common Good of the planet.[5]

For their part, the leaders and the executives can accelerate this transformation:

- by founding the purpose of the company, not on profit alone, but on its creativity and its ability to ensure sustainable economic and technical progress
- by placing ethics at the heart of strategic decisions and behaviour
- by opening themselves up to discussions on the Common Good of the planet and actively contributing in their fields of activity.

A new balance must be sought between the three roles that constitute the leadership function:

- The entrepreneur-businessman, key-actor of economic creation (*entrepreneurship*)
- The leader, bringer of ethical values (*leadership*)
- The citizen engaged in the political debate and the pursuit of the Common Good (*statesmanship*).

---

[5] de Woot, Ph., *Should Prometheus Be Bound?*, Palgrave-MacMillan, 2005 and 2009. *Responsabilité sociale de l'entreprise. Faut-il enchaîner Prométhée?* Economica, 2005.

If we want to avoid current failures turning into global catastrophes, it is imperative to get the economy under the aegis of ethics and politics. The surge of our development model risks driving us against a wall, or "to the abyss", as the most realistic would probably say.

To the horseman who passed through a village at full gallop and could no longer control his runaway horse, a resident asked, "Where are you running to like that?" to which the horseman replied: "Ask the horse!"[6] Nowadays we have to find back "our mastery's mastery"

Can the leaders transform the company and the system that it leads without being transformed themselves?

At a time when we talk about emotional and spiritual intelligence, let us remember that Christian anthropology, since its inception, offers a vision of man that includes these dimensions. This vision can go beyond mere rationality to open up the less tangible but more profound realities of the heart and the soul.

Do we use enough of the extraordinary power of transformation that our spirituality can give us when it is lived out in all aspects of our life?

This essay wishes to play an active part in the debate struck up by the International Christian Union of Business Executives (UNIAPAC) on the company and the necessary modification of the economic system. It incorporates and expands upon some topics and passages of my book on corporate social responsibility[7], against the backdrop of a more Christian and spiritual perspective and by presenting them in a more polemic way. It is also directed at a more specific audience. It is written as dialogue with numerous teams of Christian executives and leaders, with their study centres and their national and regional associations. More generally, it is directed at all those who are interested in the aims of the economy and the necessary evolution of our current system. It does not claim to give lessons. If some questions seem critical, they are not directed at those who question and seek, but to those who insist on separating their professional commitment from their spiritual commitment.

---

[6] Ringlet, G., *L'évangile d'un libre penseur (The Gospel and the free thinker)*, Paris, Albin Michel, 1998.

[7] de Woot, Ph., *op. cit.*

This little book does not fit into the tradition of academic or scientific work. Its intention is to sound alarm bells and to outline some possible ways forward. The preconception is that of quotes and maxims, "pearls of wisdom" that shed light without lengthy explanation. These texts are intended to give depth to the thinking. They often come from a universal and age-old wisdom, of this old body of experience of Mankind, of its most acute questions and of a revelation that should not cease to enlighten us.

CHAPTER 1

ON THE EDGE OF THE ABYSS OR THE THREAT OF UNREASON

> See, I offer you today life and good, death and misfortune ... I offer you life or death, the blessing or the curse. Choose therefore life so that you and your descendants may live ... If you do not obey the Lord your God (if you do not give an ethical dimension to development) you will be cursed in the city and cursed in the country. Your basket and your kneading trough will be cursed. The fruit of your womb will be cursed, and the crops of your land, and the calves of your herds and the lambs of your flocks ... The Lord will send on you curses, confusion and rebuke in everything you put your hand to until you are destroyed and come to sudden ruin, until he has destroyed you from the Land you are entering to possess. The sky over your head will be bronze, the ground beneath you iron ... The Lord will cause you to be defeated before your enemies ... He will afflict you with madness, blindness and confusion of mind ... *(Deuteronomy, 28:15–28)*

By disassociating economic activity from politics and ethics, we are doing the wrong thing.

Blinded by the brilliant achievements of our economic system, we do not see that insanity looms over us and that once again barbarity threatens us.

Systemic drifts and deviations

All recent analyses of our development model revealed major dysfunctions and unintended effects that call into question its long term effectiveness and legitimacy. But it is necessary to push the sole economic analysis further to show the extent of the crisis that threatens us and the urgency of significant reform.

The company being the archetype of economic and technical creativity, it was long believed that its action *automatically* served the

Common Good thanks to the virtues of the market and of its famous "invisible hand". Nowadays, this belief is clearly called into question.

Globalisation, the advances in technological sciences and the lack of global regulation confer the power to act without precedent upon the economic system. It exerts this power according to its own criteria: profitability, competitiveness, market share. In the absence of global regulation, this approach tends to become dominant and imposes a development model on us that has no other purpose than its own effectiveness and dynamism. Led by instrumental logic alone, this model becomes more and more ambiguous and paradoxical: never has our ability to create richness been so great and never has the number of poor people been so high; never has our scientific and technical knowledge been so broad and never has the planet been so threatened; never has the need for economic governance been so compelling and never have nation states been so disarmed.

All the while ensuring economic growth, unprecedented in human history, our model races on, pollutes, excludes, and brings about incidences of domination, social injustice and deconstruction.

It begs the question whether the current model is still politically and morally acceptable without profound changes.

We may even ask ourselves if we have completely blinded ourselves to the failings of this, if we are party to these overall malfunctions and whether they lead us towards the irrational.

Our model generates systemic risks which are not clearly desired, which are difficult to measure if not to anticipate, and whose consequences can jeopardise the social balance, the methods of control and regulation, the institutions and the planet itself. We are in a high risk society that requires us to force ourselves to question, and to take more responsibility to invent new methods of regulation and governance.[1]

Does a Christian vision of the company not oblige us to become aware of the fact that this system, despite its brilliant achievements,

---

[1] See Beck, U., *La société du risque. Sur la voie d'une autre modernité*, Paris, Flammarion Champs, 2003. Risk Society: Towards a new modernity, Sage Publications, London, 1992, London. See also Beck, U., and Giddens, A., *Reflexive Modernization*, Stanford University Press, 1994.

is reaching its limits and could lead us into up against a brick wall? The explosion of the financial bubble has shown how fragile it was, how little we knew and how devastating the effects could be on the weakest.

All too often, we take refuge behind the simplistic argument that our model is the best possible and that all others have shown their inability to generate wealth as effectively. It has flaws but they can be corrected, and moreover it continues to improve, etc...

A Christian leader among the most committed, worthy of the greatest admiration and who seeks more than most leaders to correct the human foibles of our model, however, writes this:

> The only thing of which I am convinced is that the system of the market economy is the best that man had been able to develop. So, if there are weaknesses today, that are indeed less than that at the time of Karl Marx, we only have one choice, and that is to continue to improve it.[2]

He does so and it is fundamental and it is wonderful. But our system which becomes global, does it not, on a worldwide scale, have infinitely more defects than at the time of Marx? Some companies, it is true, have been humanised, but the system as a whole ...?

As well as a genuine commitment in the company, should we not make a more objective and radical criticism of the system itself if we want the Christian commitment to further influence its transformation? Should we not have the courage to call things by their name rather than risk being locked into an optimism that could be misleading?

This is what we have tried to illustrate in the following lines.

Folly watches over us...

> There is a kind of folly that the Furies unleash from Hell each time that they release their snakes and toss the ardour of war to the hearts of mortals, the insatiable thirst for gold...

---

[2] Ouimet, J.-R., 'Tout vous a été confié'. Entretiens avec Yves Semen ('All that has been entrusted to you'. Interviews with Yves Semen), Presses de la Renaissance, Paris, 2008.

> The other kind of folly bears no similarity... It arises each time that a sweet illusion liberates the soul of its tiresome worries.[3]

Surely the first folly is **to have disassociated the economic activity from politics and ethics**? And by that, to have locked ourselves in *the sweet illusion* of "unidimensional thought"?

Economic globalisation is advancing faster than global governance. It escapes the nation states and gradually imposes its logic on the entire planet. This delay in economic policy leads to a sort of public helplessness to drive real development strategy and to democratically debate societal issues of globalisation. It is as if it was binding on States, not even leaving them the freedom to choose the type of market economy which suits their country. Thus the Anglo-Saxon model, more financial and less social, tends to gain ground on a more human model, like the social market economy or Rhineland model.[4]

Our economic model operates according to the logic of means and not ends: it involves maximising the use of rare resources and the resulting profits. This system is amoral. It does not, *in itself*, give any indication other than that of solvent markets. Without an ethical or political framework at the global level, it is only guided by its instrumental logic. Under the respectable appearance of dynamism and efficiency in a world open to changes, liberal globalisation also hides a radical ideology. It involves, quite simply, an all too absolutist belief in the efficiency of the markets and of an almost visceral distrust in respect of public intervention and international regulation of economic relations. What a mistake it is to think of the market economy as a self-regulating process that *automatically* contributes to the Common Good! It also entails a truncated conception of the role of the company of which, according to Milton Friedman, *the only social responsibility would be the enrichment of the shareholder*.

This, as we see every day, drives the actors in the system to behave unreasonably while the economic theory presents them as rational beings.

---

[3] Erasme, *Eloge de la folie (The Praise of Folly)*, Flammarion, Paris, 1964.

[4] Albert, M., *Capitalisme contre capitalisme (Capitalism against capitalism)*, Seuil, Paris, 1991.

What madness to believe that globalisation could smoothly disperse this market logic to the entire planet, without taking sufficient account of political, cultural and institutional differences, a bit like a steamroller!

> The image of the Kingdom is the bearer of another globalisation, that of the universality of human destiny, that of St Paul, where there is neither Greek, nor Jew, and when, according to St Matthew "all nations will be gathered before Him". However, it must be clear, that today globalisation means the universalisation of capitalist market relations, that which Paul VI called the imperialism of money (Popularum Progressio), where the strongest win, where profitability is the dominant logic, where shareholder interests preside over the basic needs of Mankind, where the function of the economy deviates from its meaning, that of providing the basis for the physical, cultural and spiritual development of all human beings around the world, to become solely the production of an added value and finally, where a minority accounts for more than 80% of global income, while hundreds of millions of human beings live in poverty.[5]

Is another folly not **to have left** *finance* **to dominate the economy** and subordinate entrepreneurship to the vagaries of speculation? *Irrational exuberance* is just one recent example of this.

Financial capitalism overlooks the real economy now and leads it in a speculative race where money serves to create more money without investing in the production of goods or of services which are useful to people.

> The requirement of return, financial in origin, first infiltrated the whole of the economy to then become omnipresent in society and even in the culture of daily life. This development has today led Western societies to a paradoxical situation where they have lost their freedom because their present is actually constrained by the requirements imposed by their own financial future, such as has been articulated by the architects of loanback pensions and proposed by the advocates of

---

[5] Houtart, F., 'Une mondialisation de la justice, de l'amour et de la vie' ('Globalisation of justice, love and life'), *Homélie*, Fête patronale de l'UCL, Feb 3, 2003.

"shareholder value". This "bright future" is proving to be as fanciful as if it were proposed by the communist utopia.[6]

With speculation bearing on the spirit of the company, we let ourselves slide towards a casino economy where behaviours become, all too often, those of greed and excess: delusional requirements of profitability and growth, dishonesty over figures, dishonesty over products (financial products, after tobacco, fertilisers, seeds . . .), excesses in external growth strategies, and excesses in executives' pay . . .

If finance claims to be its own goal and no longer led only by the exclusive desire for profit, it loses its head.[7]

Economic development proves to be artificial and harmful if it relies on financial "miracles" to support an artificial growth related to excessive consumption.[8]

The ethos of efficiency emancipated from the authority of morality has gradually promoted the increasingly brutal expression of greed[9]

Once more, our system is prostrating itself before the golden calf!

Can one contribute to the establishment of the Kingdom without fighting this excessive financial domination? This is a difficult issue for a business leader but all the more relevant in light of the devastation caused by speculation.

They covet fields and seize them, and houses, and take them,
They defraud a man of his home, a fellow-man of his inheritance.
(Micah 2:2)

---

[6] Dembinski, P.H., 'Finance servante ou finance trompeuse?' ('Helpful finance or misleading finance?'), Report of the *Observatoire de la Finance*, Paris Desclée de Brouwer, 2008.

[7] Conseil pour les questions familiales et sociales de la Conférence des Evêques de France, *Réflexion sur la crise financière (Reflection on the financial crisis)*, Oct 8, 2008 (Council for Family and Social Affairs, Conference of Bishops of France).

[8] *Caritas in veritate, 68.*

[9] Dembinski, P.H., *op. cit.*

Woe to you who add house to house
and join field to field
till no space is left
and you live alone in the land. *(Isaiah 5:8)*

...They trample on the heads of the poor as upon the dust of the
    ground
and deny justice to the oppressed. *(Amos 2:7)*

Woe to him who piles up stolen goods – how long must this go on?
and makes himself wealthy by extortion!
Will not your debtors suddenly arise?
Will they not wake you up and make you tremble?
Then you will become their victim! *(Habakkuk 2:6–7)*

Another folly is to give an economic system which is decoupled from politics and ethics **the near-exclusive power to seize scientific developments** and to immediately transform them into competitive technologies. All that is made possible by science must be applied immediately and inserted into the market system. Science thus becomes the hostage and the decisive weapon of economic power without ethics or any real control.

This brings us back to the ambiguous nature of technology and possible applications of science. Technical progress will be beneficial or malevolent according to the use that will be made of it.

More than ever, one must remember that today this use is more about the order of means than that of ends.

With his ingenuity that surpasses all expectations, man progresses towards evil or good. *(Sophocles)*

A few examples will suffice in illustration of this point.

Biogenetics promises abundant harvests, the healing of incurable diseases, the prolonging of our lives without much decay... But it also stirs the ghost of genetic manipulations with unpredictable consequences touching on the very nature of Mankind and all living species.

Nuclear technology detects illnesses better, cures certain cancers and protects food, mail and medical instruments from any contamination ... It provides a cheap source of energy, which does not pollute the atmosphere, but its waste represents a long-term threat which has not been controlled to this day. It can become a formidable instrument of deterrence and destruction at the hands of rulers and the military, but also of blackmail and terror at the hands of extremists or "Rogue States". Man now faces the possibility of destroying his own species.

The internet and the media open up an incredible world of information, interactive communication, exchange, debate and education. They could create this "noosphere", so dear to Teilhard de Chardin, and facilitate the emergence of a world united in its diversity. But they also carry within them all of the possible facets of a world subject to information overload, simplifications, ratings, insularity within narrow specialisations or deluded identities. They can also amplify global threats to safety, criminal networks and the *ad nauseam* broadcasting of violent and pornographic images. They also oblige us to completely rethink certain basic concepts such as the respect for private life that already no longer enjoys protection from the use of personal data for marketing purposes.

In his essay on culture, Georges Steiner has clearly stated the problem.[10]

Unlike art, science works by accumulation and its development becomes exponential. It gradually escapes the democratic debate. By their scale and pace, science and technology have acquired a particular dynamism and an independence that may lead them down dangerous paths.

> Any definition of a post-classical civilisation must learn to sit alongside scientific knowledge and with the world of mathematic and symbolic languages. For they alone possess the absolute power: in the facts as well as in the fever of progress that defines us ... It makes sense that science and technology have caused irreparable environmental damage, and economic imbalance and moral laxity ...
>
> However, in spite of confused and bucolic criticism of writers such as Thoreau and Tolstoy, no-one seriously doubted that it had to go this way.

---

[10] Steiner, G., *Dans le château de Barbe Bleue. Note pour une redéfinition de la culture (In the castle of BlueBeard. Note for a redefinition of culture)*, Paris, Seuil, 1973.

It enters in this attitude, most often irrational, partly of a blind, mercantile instinct, an immeasurable thirst for comfort and consumption. But also a far more powerful mechanism: the belief rooted in the heart of the Western personality, at least since Athens, that intellectual inquiry must proceed, that such momentum is consistent with nature and meritorious in itself...

Science and technology progress faster than our political, legal and ethical thinking. They present new questions that take us completely by surprise. The distrust of the citizen regarding GMOs, genetic engineering or nuclear power is therefore understandable.

What must be underlined at this stage is the danger that we risk encountering if we hesitate in integrating scientific and technical progress in an ethical and political vision of our planet's future, and if we are to leave the techno-sciences to their own momentum and market logic. The techno-sciences, when grasped by an economic system with no clear *raison d'être* and free to impose on us its own choices, could lock us in a world of which the *Brave New World* would only be a children's tale.

> The new sciences flood us with information about what we can do... but it does not follow that it should be done, even less that we should do all that is within our ability.[11] For good people, should all that can be done, be done? *(Cicero)*

Is it not also folly **to let our universities slide into the technical deviation** which imposes on them the increasing emphasis of "hard" sciences and methods to the detriment of a real questioning of their meaning and purposes for Mankind as well as a little deeper anthropological thought? This applies to all disciplines but in particular, as we shall see later on, to economy and management.

Science is only one mode of knowledge available to man. It only delivers to us the reality that it can discover by its observation methods, measures and experimentation. It says nothing about the uniqueness of individuals, nothing about meaning and purpose,

---

[11] Moussé, J., *Fondements d'une éthique professionnelle (Foundations of professional ethics)*, Paris, Les Editions d'organisation, 1989.

nothing serious about moral suffering, evil and destiny. These essential questions are outside of its domain. They are, however, at the heart of our political choices and the construction of the future.

> It is not scientific knowledge that is in question, but the current ideology that considers it to be the only sort of knowledge... Knowledge has been diverted from the living action, it has become the preserve of science... The praxis of science conceives truth as outside the ontological sphere of the living truth.[12]
>
> Among the Greeks and the Romans, the admiration of moral and political knowledge was brought to a sort of cult status. Today, we only have high regard for the physical sciences, we are solely occupied by them, and political good and evil are, among us, a feeling rather than a subject of knowledge.[13]

Here is what F. Flahault, a modern anthropologist, has to say[14]:

> The model of rational action, is that of thought-out action, based on the knowledge of cause and effect, of means and ends. The world of things is clearly distinguished from that of human relations, willingly deemed "irrational", "emotional" or "affective"...
>
> This vision of man and the world tends to reinforce itself... and scientific knowledge has experienced extraordinary growth. As a general rule, what Mankind achieves falls short of its dreams. The suffering which results from human relations (armed conflict, discord, violence, exploitation, poverty, disruption, instability and political errors, etc.) brings us face to face with our limits and our failures. The domain of natural sciences and technology is on the contrary the only one where the performance of the human mind goes beyond the predictions made one or two centuries ago... An enormous and growing gap is extending between our knowledge of the material world and that of the world of human relationships.

---

[12] Henry, M., *La Barbarie (Barbarity)*, Grasset, 1987.
[13] Montesquieu, Ch. de, 'Considérations sur les causes de la grandeur des Romains et de leur décadence' ('Consderations of the causes of Roman grandeur and decadence').
[14] Flahault, F., *Le crépuscule de Prométhée: Contribution à une histoire de la démesure humaine (The twilight of Prometheus: Contribution to a history of human excesses)*, Mille et une nuits, 2008.

All those who appear to be mad are mad, and so are half of those who do not appear to be so. *(Gracian)*

The Earth reels with its entire load. I say to the foolish: Stop your foolishness *(Psalm 75, 4–5.)*

> My people are fools ... they are senseless children; they have no
>   understanding...
> I looked at the earth, and it was formless,
> at the heavens, and their light was gone.
> I looked at the mountains, and they were quaking;
> and all the hills were swaying.
> I looked, and there were no people;
> every bird in the sky had flown away.
> I looked, and the fruitful land was a desert,
> all its towns lay in ruins...
> The whole land will be ruined... *(Jeremiah 4:22–27)*

And barbarity threatens us ...

In quickening our step, our development model begins to destroy **the planet** by exhausting resources, water and soil pollution, and global warming.

> The earth will become desolate
> because of its inhabitants,
> as the result of their deeds. *(Micah 7:13)*

> You will eat but not be satisfied;
> you will store up but save nothing,
> because what you save I will give to the sword;
> you will plant but not harvest;
> you will press the olives but not use the oil on yourselves,
> you will crush the grapes but not drink the wine. *(Micah 6:14–15)*

The consequences of global warming will become dramatic: cyclones, tornadoes, tsunamis, desertification, destruction of food supplies, famine, population displacement... And it is the poorest that will pay the highest price!

The Intergovernmental Panel on Climate Change (IPCC) tells us that from now until 2050, the displacement of 150 million people is likely.[15]

Can one still halt this forecasted apocalypse or is trying to adapt ourselves to the inevitable cataclysms all that remains for us to do?

Expectations in this area are becoming increasingly dark.

"Quietly in public, loudly in private, climate scientists everywhere are saying the same thing: it's over. The years in which more than 2°C of global warming could have been prevented have passed, the opportunities squandered by denial and delay. On current trajectories we'll be lucky to get away with 4°C. Mitigation (limiting greenhouse gas pollution) has failed; now we must adapt to what nature sends our way. If we can."[16]

"The Intergovernmental Panel on Climate Change says that "global mean temperature changes greater than 4°C above 1990–2000 levels" would "exceed... the adaptive capacity of many systems". At this point there's nothing you can do, for instance, to prevent the loss of ecosystems, the melting of glaciers and the disintegration of major ice sheets...

And it doesn't stop there. The IPCC also finds that, above 3°C of warming, the world's vegetation will become "a net source of carbon" [emitting more CO_2 than it takes in]. This is just one of the climate feedbacks triggered by a high level of warming. Four degrees might take us inexorably to 5°C or 6°C: the end for humans and for just about everything."[17]

If one considers the degradation of the seas, mere chapter headings are enough to make one shudder: pollution and acidification of waters, over-fishing and rapid disappearance of fish stocks, changes in wind patterns and ocean currents, destruction of coral reefs and mass extinction of the species that live within them...

Opening the World Ocean Conference in May 2009, the President of Indonesia said that it was *a question of life or death for the community of nations.*

---

[15] GIEC, 2007, *Assessing key vulnerabilities and the risk from climate change.*
[16] Montbiot, G., *The Guardian*, March 17, 2009.
[17] *Ibid.*

Deforestation, acid rain, photochemical smog, the extinction of species, depletion of groundwater... where are we headed?

> There will be signs in the sun, moon and stars. On the earth, nations will be in anguish and perplexity at the roaring and tossing of the sea. Men will faint from terror, apprehensive of what is coming on the world, for the heavenly bodies will be shaken.
>
> *(Luke 21:25–26)*

Despite the development of entire regions, our economic model increases **inequality and alienation**, it destroys rural farmers inhabiting impoverished regions and increases their dependence (for example, by trying to impose "sterile" seeds upon them). Today, 1.3 billion people struggle to survive on less than one dollar a day. In the words of John-Paul II, this represents *something of a gigantic development of the biblical parable of the rich who feast and of the poor Lazarus*.[18]

In the absence of a global regulation, the phenomena of economic and technical power most often play out at the expense of the poorest countries. Supporters of a deregulated world forget that *between the rich and the poor, between the strong and the weak, it is liberty that oppresses and the law that liberates (Lacordaire)*.

> You who turn justice into bitterness and cast righteousness to the ground
>
> *(Amos 5:7)*

When this power is exercised in more or less equal competitive games, it contributes to growth and development. Alternatively, as respect many developing countries, the competition is wholly unequal. We impose a model on them, ours, to which they are unprepared and which locks them in a position of weakness. International organisations, like the IMF, the World Bank or the WTO, push them – or oblige them – to open their borders, prevent them from implementing any industrial policy worthy of this name, to instead practice budgetary restraint and financial orthodoxy within

---

[18] Berten, I., *op. cit.*

a purist and hard-line monetarism. Some radical critics argue that WTO rules could have been written with the intention of making all industrial and technological policies that have succeeded in the capitalist governments of East and South East Asia in developing local industries henceforth illegal.[19] We thus condemn them to remain producers of raw materials whose terms of trade continue to fluctuate.

> Should you not know justice?
> you who hate good and love evil;
> who tear the skin from my people
> and the flesh from their bones;
> who eat my peoples' flesh,
> strip off their skin
> and break their bones,
> who chop them up like meat for the pan,
> like flesh for the pot. *(Micah 3:1–3)*

Agricultural policies in Europe and the United States have long been sad examples of domination and inequality: every year, rich countries have spent huge sums on subsidising their agricultural exports, seriously damaging poor countries by an artificial depression of prices that further aggravated productivity inequalities.

All this taints, with obvious hypocrisy, the very idea of the market economy that we preach as a truth of faith that we impose because we are the strongest, and we systematically falsify to our profit.

> Woe to those who make unjust laws, to those who issue
>   oppressive decrees,
> to deprive the poor of their rights
> and withhold justice from the oppressed of my people,
> making widows their prey
> and robbing the fatherless. *(Isaiah 10:1–2)*

Should one mention here the freedom to speculate on a global scale about the price of raw food staples such as rice or wheat? To submit

---

[19] Wade, R.H., London School of Economics, *FT*, Ausut 29, 2003.

the hunger of the poor to the financial games of the rich is a terrible illustration of the barbarity of our financial system.

> Skimping the measure, boosting the price, and cheating with dishonest scales. *(Amos 8:5)*

> You trample on the poor
> and force him to give you grain.
> though you have built stone mansions,
> you will not live in them;
> though you have planted lush vineyards,
> you will not drink their wine.
> For I know how many are your offences
> and how great your sins.
> You oppress the righteous and take bribes,
> you deprive the poor of justice in their courts. *(Amos 5:11–12)*

Our model also begins to destroy **the cultural diversity** of the planet and to distribute a culture of immediacy, channel hopping, consumerism left, right and centre, and violence. The concentration and the power of multimedia groups have become as they say today *more powerful than governments, NGOs and educational institutions* (An executive at Time Warner).

They already occupy the field of leisure and entertainment.

For Pascal, entertainment consisted of *dancing, playing the lute, singing, writing poetry, running the ring, etc ... of fighting, of making oneself a king, without thinking of what it means to be king and to be man.*[20] Today, it has not changed much but the entertainment has become more and more pervasive and it is now the dominant part of a mass culture largely managed by the media, a mixture of music, images, shared rhythms and also shared games, of "Reality TV" and variety shows where digital applause rivals the canned laughter. The concern is not so much about the entertainment itself than the fact that it is guided by economic actors for whom profit is the sole purpose.

These media groups are gradually moving these variety shows towards that which they believe to be education (*edutainment*). If we leave American groups to dominate the scene too much, our

---

[20] Pascal, B., *Pensées*, in *Œuvres (Thoughts in Works)*, Paris, Gallimard, 1950.

grandchildren may be introduced to Iliad and the Odyssey by Mickey Mouse and Donald Duck. Is this the world that we want?

One will object that the Internet will allow this pitfall to be avoided. Do not underestimate the power of these private actors that will obviously be very present across all networks.

The primary threat in this area comes from the importance of advertising. This problem affects most television channels, above all private channels. These often become the Mecca for transforming culture into a commodity as advertising budgets have a decisive influence on the choice of programmers.

In a society driven by the market, advertising plays a disproportionate role. In many cases, *making television is, in between each advertisement, about creating sufficiently attractive content for the advertising material to have an audience.*[21]

> There are several ways of talking about television. But in a "business" perspective, let us be realistic: on a basic level, the job of TF1, is to help Coca Cola, for example, to sell its product. However for an advertisement to be seen, the viewer's brain must be available. Our broadcasts are designed to make it available: that is to say to entertain, to relax and prepare it between two messages. What we sell to Coca Cola, is available human brain time.[22]

The ratings tend to become the dominant criterion and the most destructive of a cultural direction worthy of its name. Advertising invades everything and takes undue prominence in the collective imagination. In order to sell, it sometimes uses the most dubious and questionable means. Hence one may ask what purpose do ethical advertising codes serve.

Some agencies comply with nothing. On behalf of the very legitimate freedom of expression, they use and manipulate, often without respect, the values, situations and the fragility of youth. A recent bank advertisement pushed children to demand more money

---

[21] De Vezins, V., *Le Figaro*, August 2002.

[22] Le Lay, P., in *Les associés d'EIM, Les dirigeants face au changement (Partners of EIM, Leaders faced with change)*, Les Editions du Huitième Jour, Paris, 2004.

from their parents and to do so by contract because you never know when Alzheimer's may set in …!

An advertising poster for a car manufacturer used an image that resembles one used by the Internet to attract paedophile tourists to Thailand – three young girls face on and a young man with his back to us – as well as the following slogan: "Come and try out the little new ones". Is it any wonder that this disgusts some people and that they question the growing barbarity of market ideology without purpose or morality? "That these new thinkers, these behemoths of communication, that these guarantors of the world market and morality have little regard for what is in their heads and that the sick people that have conceived of and invented this shit advert in their hearts and minds, pay damages to victims' parents."[23]

Let us return to **science**. Some recent scientific researches ask questions that our weak ethical thinking is unable to deal with. This could have immeasurable consequences.

> In succession we open the doors to the castle of Blue Beard because "they are there", because each leads to the next, according to the intensification process by which the mind defines itself…We pursue the reality that leads us…The real issue is whether to persist in some research if society and the human mind, in their current state of development, could bear to know the truth. It is possible – and already, dilemmas that history has never known before are arising – it is therefore possible that the next door opens up to the realities which are essentially contrary to our psychological balance and to our meagre moral reserves…Who will say that what awaits us is not a trap, if the link between speculative thinking and problems of survival that our civilisation is based on is not about to break?… The "positive truths" that lie behind the laws of science are transformed into a darker dungeon than that of Piranesi, a "carcere" where the future is held. It is these facts and not the man who determine the course of history…I expect that the last door of the castle will be pushed, even if it opens, or perhaps because it opens, out onto realities beyond the reach of human authority and understanding.[24]

---

[23] Ide, P., *Venez les essayer les nouvelles petites (Come and try out the new little ones)*, La Libre Belgique, May 22, 2003.

[24] Steiner, G., *op.cit.*

The influence of the techno-sciences was often beneficial to humanity. But, at the same time, they open the door to the worst apocalypses such as nuclear wars or genetic engineering that could damage or destroy man. For François Jacobs, winner of the Prix Nobel for Medicine,[25] genetic engineering creates irrational fantasies because *it seems to touch upon the supernatural. It brings back the mists of time, some of the myths rooted in the fears of man. It recalls the terror that provokes in us the vision of monsters, the reluctance associated with the idea of hybrids and beings united against nature. The genetic knowledge calls to mind evil knowledge, the very kind of forbidden knowledge... It became subject to the greatest accusation brought against science: to give biologists the power to debase and enslave the human body and mind.*

For François Jacobs, these fantasies keep us from dealing calmly with the fundamental question of risks and possible misuse but make it even more urgent.

For example, we are on the point today, for therapeutic purposes, of authorising the creation of "chimeras", mixtures of human and animal, and the age-old dread of Mankind.

Rampant dehumanisation

The pace of economic and technical change accelerates under the effect of global competition. We have entered an absurd race whose speed is imposed by the dynamism of companies and competitive games.

This pace is often faster than that of political, civil and institutional society. Our administrative, education and social systems adapt with increasing difficulty. This shift creates a growing danger of inequality, exclusion, unemployment and social breakdown. We are beginning to run the risk of seeing the system grind people down.

More profoundly, an existential approach to our economic system[26] shows that it is not only growth, innovation, progress and expansion, but it is also a force of alienation, an absurd dynamic

---

[25] Jacobs, F., *La souris, la mouche et l'homme (The mouse, the fly and man)*, Editions Odile Jacobs, Paris, 1997.
[26] Arnsperger, Ch., *Critique de l'existence capitaliste (Critique of the capitalist existence)*, Cerf, Paris, 2005.

where the true meaning of life is lost. The obsession with productivity, the headlong rush of competition, the loss of autonomy, the collective loss of values, lead us to think just as Rimbaud that *true life is elsewhere*. The anthropological structures of life are distorted by the social structures of economic action. Far from responding to our aspirations and our deepest fears, the economic system offers only an "existential clogging".

> The economy today has become the existentially inauthentic social place...
>
> Social order is built, not on ontology, nor on a common meaningful design, but indeed in one form or another of the balance of forces...
>
> By its very logic, capitalism perpetuates the commodification of the world by excessive consumerism, market speculation, financial flows without social ties, the exacerbation of the spirit of competition, the instrumentalisation of human relations...
>
> Capitalist society is incapable of realising the ideal of a just society on the ground where it will lay... It prevents the emergence of a genuine existential rationale.[27]
>
> The barbarian is the man who is unfaithful to his own kind.[28]

In the first discussion on development, Moses highlights the importance of the submission of economic development to the imperatives of the Common Good under pain of curse: ... *the Lord will smite thee with madness, blindness and stupidity of mind.*

Prometheus, fastened to his rock, is afflicted by the same stupor. In a great cry of pride, he cries: *I eliminated for men the agony of death!* Hubris leads him to madness: *That lightning burns me with its flame, that the roaring thunder from the bowels of the earth and that Zeus unleashes united forces, upsets the world and opens it up to chaos, nothing will make me flinch.* So the chorus replies: *You have not learned wisdom, Prometheus, your heart is hardened; the pride of fools is little strength.*

Excess, arrogance, madness. One may wonder whether or not our development model leads us on this slippery slope and whether it is

---

[27] Arnsperger, Ch., *op. cit.*

[28] Mattei, J.-F., *La barbarie intérieure (Internal barbarity)*, PUF, 2006.

time to reflect once more on the old theme of human madness and barbarity that so often accompanies it.

> So justice is far from us, and righteousness does not reach us.
> We look for light, but all is darkness; for brightness, but we
>   walk in deep shadows.
> Like the blind we grope along the wall,
> feeling our way like men without eyes.
> At midday we stumble as if it were twilight,
> among the strong, we are like the dead (*Isaiah 59:9–10*).

Is the role of Christian leaders and executives not also to denounce the growing deviations of our economic model and its drift toward folly, insanity and the new forms of barbarity? Is it not time to further advocate the transformation of the entire system?

Do we adequately fulfil this role?

Today when one rereads certain reassuringly optimistic, soothing and conservative discussions, one might doubt it. It is not by playing Doctor Pangloss that we will salt the earth. Let us be aware of *the easy optimism of the conscienceless prophets* (unidimensional thinking) *and, behind them, of the choir paid of those who follow them.*[29] To serve as a leaven and to help rise the dough, there must be a clear will as well as the courage for basic questioning.

Today, the "oracles of doom" are probably closer to reality, and thus more useful, than the conformist vision of certain leaders. From 2008, the crisis already forced 155 millions of people into poverty. Some European expectations[30] tell us that this is just the beginning, that we could be entering a greater period of depression than that of 1929, that there is a severe risk of social chaos and political instability with the potential to lead to a third world war. One wonders whether the apocalyptic warnings do not speak better than words of saintly hypocrites praising our present situation and of that which can happen to our development model if we do not deeply change.

---

[29] Zweig, S., *Le monde d'hier (The world of yesterday)*, Paris, Belfond, 1993.
[30] Global Europe Anticipation Bulletin no. 33, Europe 2020.

...there will be great distress in the land...

...know that its desolation is near...

...nations will be in anguish and perplexity at the roaring and tossing of the sea...

...men will faint from terror, apprehensive of what is coming...

...Be always on the watch, and pray that you may be able to escape all that is about to happen... *(Luke 21:20–36)*

Are we not faced with a drift so serious that it imposes more radical ethical and political choices on us?

> ... *Be very careful, then, how you live – not as unwise but as wise, making the most of every opportunity, because the days are evil.* (Paul, *Ephesians*, 5:15–16)

> See, I am setting before you the way of life and the way of death. Choose life. *(Jeremiah, 21, 8)*

> Leave your foolish ways and you will live, walk in the way of understanding. *(Proverbs, 9, 6)*

Should we not today *venture to anticipate a different world?*[31]

To commit oneself, one must be fully aware of the reality. One must announce the changes to come, scream loudly, and awaken the economic actors. Why are Christian leaders not more prophetic?

Let us stop kidding ourselves. We are on the edge of the abyss. We are headed towards increasingly serious crises whose consequences will be disastrous. Let us stop following one another like sheep and bleating in chorus the merits of an unbridled market economy and, above all, participating in it without trying to transform it deeply. Let us commit ourselves but do not underestimate the power of the system or the cynicism of its masters. Less than a year after having triggered a global crisis, the financiers return to their perverse practices and the public authorities seem unable to force them to change. Wall Street and the City flout the G20 guidelines and we are left to take part in a casino economy!

---

[31] Berten, I., *op. cit.*

The conservative leaders make me think of *these people who, with big eyes, see the hail coming and pray to the sky that it does not fall on their land. Who dreams of turning it around? (Demosthenes)*

The most enlightened business leaders often clear their consciences by promoting new practices of social responsibility. It is a step in the right direction but it is the entire system that must change deeply and as long as the reformers will not reach critical mass, practices or isolated examples will not continue to serve as an alibi for those who do nothing.

Will we be able transform our development model quickly enough and what role will Christian leaders play in this? Or will we maintain an excessive reliance on a system that we will still believe to be capable of self regulation?

> Man casts himself too flattering a glance to recognise his wrong and to free himself of it. *(Psalm 35)*

Will we be *victims of a genetic oddity that gave us the intelligence and skill to conquer the world, but not enough wisdom to manage the fruit of our victories?*[32]

> The old is dying, the new does not yet see the day. In this interregnum monsters rise up. *(Gramsci)*[33]

---

[32] de Duve, Ch., *Génétique du péché originel: le poids du passé sur l'avenir de la vie (Genetics of the original sinner: the weight of the past on life's future)*, Paris, Odile Jacob, 2009.

[33] Gramsci, A., *Cahiers de prison (Prison notebooks)*, Wikipedia.

CHAPTER 2

A NEW COMPANY AND A NEW SPIRIT

2-1 ENTREPRENEURSHIP AND CREATION

CO-CREATOR

Spurred on by competition and technological advances, the successful company does not content itself with the production and distribution of goods and services. It constantly renews them, makes them evolve, and creates new ones.

If one monitors successful companies over a period of five or ten years, it could be seen that not a single one had failed to adapt, transform or renew itself. Each one would have evolved and innovated, be it in their products, their markets, their procedures or their organisation. This reality marks their action with a dynamic and creative flavour.

Initiative and **creativity** constitute the backbone of entrepreneurship. It is what justifies its freedom and gives its activities a historic dimension.

Schumpeter highlighted this source of economic development.[1] For him, the competition that really counts is the competition for new goods, new techniques, new supply sources, new types of organisation... The driving force was mainly the individual entrepreneur, a rare character with specific qualities: the *vision* of potential progress, energy and an *appetite for risk* sufficient to implement it and a power of *conviction* capable of bringing him the necessary support and resources.

Today, it is not only the individual entrepreneur or businessman who creates innovation. The company has taken over a large part of this role and now ensures this type of creativity in a collective

---

[1] Schumpeter, J., *The Theory of Economic Development*, Cambridge (Mass), The Harvard University Press, 1949.

and systematic way. The reality of economic and technical development is that of major innovations, often implemented at the start by individual entrepreneurs and rapidly relayed by large corporations acting as "collective" entrepreneurs. Today, the names of Ford, Singer, Campbell, Solvay, Beckaert, Lafarge, Michelin, Renault... no longer refer merely to the creator-individuals who founded them, but to companies with collective capabilities that developed in themselves the qualities of the famous entrepreneurs who created them. As we shall see later on, it is on that role that they should focus on to define their *raison d'être* and found their legitimacy.

The individual or collective entrepreneur is thus, in his field, fundamentally **creative**.

In this context, defining the *raison d'être* of the company consists in giving a meaning to this creativity that could transform it into a real progress for human kind and, as Christians, bring a contribution to the advent of the Kingdom.

Christian theologians tell us that creation is unfinished and that man is responsible for its completion and its humanisation.

> A creator-God created the human creator...
>
> God created a creation in the active sense of the word: something in the process of making itself...
>
> Man was created to create... God did not create things, rather he created the creation, something that has always to invent itself and to be invented, and where man, "created creator", plays the unsurpassable role of co-creator...[2]
>
> Mankind has essentially the "power of initiative". Human freedom is this power to begin.[3]

In other words, it is by its specific function that the individual or collective entrepreneur or businessman may be associated with the Creation and the coming of the Kingdom.

---

[2] Gesché, A., *Dieu pour penser. L'homme (God to think. Man), Cerf*, 1993.

[3] Berns, T., Blésin, L., Jeanmart, G., *Du courage. Une histoire philosophique (Courage. A philisophical history)* (January 2010), Paris, Les Belles Lettres, collection "Encre Marine".

Robert Ouimet is one of the few leaders that I know, to clearly articulate this purpose when he says that the ultimate goal of the company is to *participate in the creation of God and to continue it in one's work.*[4]

In a Christian business perspective, business enterprises have a special role to play in the unfolding of the Creation. They not only provide to the human community goods and services and constantly improve them by harnessing science and technology; they also help to shape and lead organizations that can extend this work into the future.[5]

Creating material progress and building productive organizations are the primary way for business firms to share in the unfolding of the work of Creation.

Responsible for this admirable task, how can we today leave finance and speculation to dominate the real economy that is the true place of the creation of material progress and the source of social legitimacy? All civilisations have marvelled at this near-divine ability to create: the hero blacksmith in Africa, the bronze masters in China, the discoverers of the Mediterranean and of the Middle East.

How have Christian employers thought so little about the *raison d'être* of their activity to let it be so often reduced to the only financial measure of profit? How have they not succeeded in giving the social doctrine of the Church a more dynamic and enthusiastic vision of the company, based on the creation of economic progress? Still to this day, the social encyclicals talk most often of the company in terms of production of useful goods and services, which is not enough to describe the essence of their creative role. At long last, in 2012, the Pontifical Council for Justice and Peace underlines the creative specificity of the business enterprise. *Business leaders have a special role to play in the unfolding of creation – they not only provide goods and services and constantly improve them through innovating and harnessing science and technology, but they also help to shape organisations which will extend this*

---

[4] Ouimet, R., *op. cit.*

[5] "The Logic of Gift" Seminar, Rome, February 24–26, 2011 for for the Pontifical Commission for Justice and Peace.

work into the future.[6] One must look to the Greeks to hear a true song of human creativity in the economic and technical domains.

Among the founding myths of our culture, gods and creative heroes of material progress occupy an important place. The myth of Prometheus is that of the entrepreneur. He has all the characteristics of this: he *sees* the progress that fire would bring to mortals; he takes the *risk* of stealing it from the gods; he has the energy to do it and to *convince* man to use it.[7] He is a titan.

The same goes for Hephaestos (Vulcan), the god of metalcraft. He manufactures tools, weapons and jewels. He is a god.

Ulysses is a hero. His odyssey represents the commercial installation of the Greeks in the Mediterranean. He is the marketing chap of ancient history: clever, daring, enterprising... Ulysses "of a thousand tricks".

Jason pursues wealth, the Golden Fleece. The myth could not be clearer. With his Argonauts, he began to discover the Black Sea and the sources of precious metal.

Hercules is the myth of development. He is not as bright as Prometheus but he will become a god.

Finally, Icarus brings us back to full technical progress. He achieves man's ancient dream of flying like a bird.

Chained to his rock, Prometheus speaks of his work and, for the first time, in a beautiful paean, sings the spirit of enterprise and innovation

> Listen to the misery of mortels and what I have done for these delicate children that I have brought to Reason and to the force of Thought...
> One day, in the sacred stem of the narthex,

---

[6] Pontifical Council for Justice and Peace, Vocation of the Business Leader, 2012: Successful businesses identify and seek to address genuine human needs at a level of excellence using a great deal of innovation, creativity, and initiative. They produce what has been produced before but often – as in the arenas of medicine, communication, credit, food production, energy, and welfare provision – they invent *entirely new ways of meeting human needs*. And they incrementally improve their products and services, which, where they are genuinely good, improve the quality of people's lives.

[7] These are rare qualities that Schumpeter attributes to the modern businessman.

I hid the spark...
I have transmitted you, O Fire liberator,
O creative source,
Master of all arts,
Endless road that opens up for men...

Once the men had eyes to see not, they were deaf to the sound of things and, like in dream form, they waved at random in the chaos of the world. They were not building houses in the sun, they were unaware of the brick, they were not manufacturing beams nor planks and, like ants, they holed themselves up in the soil, they locked themselves in the darkness of caves. They did not foresee the return of the seasons, not daring to read in the sky neither the signs of winter, nor those of the blossoming spring, nor those of the summer that ripens the fruit. They did everything without knowing anything. Until the day where I invented for them the difficult science of the rising and setting of the stars. Then came that of numbers, queen of all knowledge. And that of the letters that one gathers, memory of every thought of man, human labourer.

Then, to relieve them of the work of the earth, I teach them to harness wild animals. The horse became obedient towards the rider, he led the chariot, he was the pride of kings. The ox bent its neck and pulled the plough. And, to cross the seas, I gave to them the boat with canvas sails...

Listen to yet more wonders. Against disease, men had nothing, they had only to die. I mixed potions, I prepared salves, their life became stronger and lasted... Finally I opened for them the treasures of the earth, they had the bronze, they had the iron, they had industry and the arts... And of a single word you can know my full work: man was poor, he was helpless. He received his genius from Prometheus. Such were my inventions. He who rescued the men did not find the path to salvation.

What an epic of economic and technical progress!
What pride those who are the protagonists should find there!
Marx himself was amazed by this ability:

in the course of a barely secular class domination, the capitalist bourgeoisie has accomplished wonders far surpassing Egyptian pyramids, Roman aqueducts and Gothic cathedrals...[8].

---

[8] Marx, K., *The Communist Manifesto*, Bruxelles, 1848.

He added:

> it has conducted expeditions that put in the shade all great invasions and
> crusades...

Another cry of praise:

> The Venetians are changers, but what genius must one have to change
> salt and dried fish into spices and silk and those into Giorgione and
> Palladio?[9]

Despite the financial overhang, the modern businessman is more
creative and innovative than ever and technical progress seems to
endlessly multiply. So why so much criticism and fears about the
companies and their leaders?

Responsible for the meaning of economic progress

It is here that we start the debate and that the real issues begin to arise.
Companies and their leaders are indeed creators.

> But a creator does not do anything. More is contained, at a basic level, in
> the word of creation than in the word of freedom alone. Here the word
> freedom means just what it means: creative responsibility, the courage
> to invent the best, the confidence to be able to achieve within a
> generous plan...
> At stake is one of the challenges of today's civilisation.
> Between alienation where I am no longer myself...and complete
> unrestricted freedom...is there no room in the end to think of true
> freedom?[10]

On the seventh day, *God retreats to make room for freedom and
responsibility.*[11]

To question the purpose of the company and the development
model that it leads, is to raise the issue of material progress, its

---

[9] Tristan, F., *Venise (Venice)*, Paris, Editions du Champ Vallon, 1984.
[10] Gesché, *op. cit.*
[11] Berten, I., *Croire en un Dieu trinitaire (Belief in a trinitarian God)*, Fidélité, 2008.

direction and its ambiguities. Man has pondered this question since the origins of civilisation.

Without an aim, economic and technical creativity is ambiguous and can be dangerous.

The temptation of excess, of arrogance, is ever present. Prometheus, the creator, understands it. He is a titan yet he is damned: the gods punish him and chain him to a rock where an eagle comes to bite at his liver every morning.

In Greek mythology, the creators of material progress are heroes and gods, but they are also cursed: Ulysses cannot return home, Jason loses his children, killed by Medea; Hercules is burned by the Tunic of Nessus, Icarus crashes and Vulcan is lame and deceived.

Why are they cursed?

Centuries on, this question rejoins our current questioning.

From the outset, this incredible series of innovations from the Neolithic era is presented in terms of progress for humans. But the other aspect of creativity would also arise, that which Aeschylus turns into tragedy: questioning the meaning, the limits and the dangers of unbridled material progress.

> My name is the seer, he who knows, Prometheus the subtle, ... he who saved mankind ... I healed man of the pangs of death.

And when the chorus of Oceanides, astonished at this extraordinary assertion, asks him: *but what remedy have you found for them*? Prometheus can only answer: *a blindfold over their eyes; blind hope*.

Blindness!

In chaining Prometheus, Aeschylus clearly questions the ambiguity of material progress decoupled from ethics and politics and of a limitless creative power.

Technical and economic creativity is not necessary beneficial for everyone.

Development through innovation is random and discontinuous, which can cause crises.

It is also brutal and dangerous since it is competitive. In the short term, it can have high social costs since it consists of an increasingly inevitable *creative destruction*.

This incessant race leads to the prevalence of a near-permanent culture of change. The new replaces the old, the past is more and more rapidly replaced by the future. The acceleration becomes such that a growing number of people can no longer adapt to the pace and are "overlooked" by progress. For them, *destruction* has prevailed over *creation*.

Let us bring into focus the dangers of a raging Promethean system that would base its legitimacy only on its technical superiority, that would be tempted by "limitlessness" and whose delusional optimism would try to dominate the world. Let us recall that if the world has received the material progress of Prometheus, this gave him neither justice nor cadency, which are the gifts of Zeus himself.[12]

Today the company possesses **considerable empowerment**. It is the company that uses most of the resources of material creation: scientific and technical knowledge, money and finance, organisational, managerial and commercial skills, information and communications networks. New technological advances constantly reinforce its capacity to innovate. New domains open up to its activity which tends nowadays to unfold in a borderless world. Increased autonomy is given to it by the very fact of globalisation. If the economy is sometimes over-regulated at national levels, the same does not apply at a global level which, up until now, is totally unregulated. This obviously favours power relations in competitive deals and the conquest of resources.

It is the existence of real power that gives an ethical and political dimension to economic activity.

If one wants the company to behave responsibly and to accept the societal consequences of its actions, it is time to extend its *raison d'être* and to implement them on other grounds than those of profit alone.

Let us permanently leave behind the narrow ideology of Milton Friedman who dared to claim that *the social responsibility of the company*

---

[12] Flahault, F., *Le crépuscule de Prométhée, Contribution à une histoire de la démesure humaine (The twilight of Prometheus: Contribution to a history of human excesses)*, Mille et une nuits, 2008.

is to maximise shareholder profit...This short-sighted approach has profoundly influenced neo-liberal thinking. We must get away from this!

Defining the *raison d'être* of the company consists in placing its role within the wider perspective of the Common Good, without which its political and moral legitimacy does not exist. Ultimately, it is to be recognised that the company is not just there for its own ends and that it serves a broader general interest. We are here in search of meaning. This should appeal to all leaders, especially Christian leaders.

We have seen that the activity of the company is essentially dynamic and creative. Through its constant innovation in the economic and technical domain, it plays a Promethean role. It is important to refocus the company on this function, rather than reduce it to a mere profit-making machine.

This allows its ethical and civic dimensions to be explicitly rendered. To question the corporate *raison d'être* and the development model that it leads is to ask the question of economic and technical creativity, of its directions and its ambiguities. To assign a purpose to the company notably consists of considering and answering the following questions:

Economic and technical creativity

- why?
- for whom?
- how?

The answers to these questions can only be ethical and political. It is the nature of those answers that will transform *creativity* into *progress* and give it its ethical and political legitimacy. Trying to give economic activity its societal *raison d'être* thus involves the insertion of specific and partial endeavours within the broader repertoire of human development.

Let us repeat that economics is merely a sub-set and that it cannot dominate society to impose on it its limited vision of progress. Other forms of progress exist in the cultural, social, political, spiritual, educational areas...If economic progress favours some of them, one cannot however pretend that it covers the whole field of human progress. We have also seen that the failings of the current system could lead to regressions and destructive situations.

We must stop pretending that there is a near-automatic convergence between current economic activity and the overall development of mankind.

We must stop insisting that personal interests alone must guide our economic behaviour and that to respond to overall challenges it is enough to trust in the technical ingenuity of man and the indications of the market.

The company will only act responsibly if it registers its specific function within an overview of human and lasting development.

In this context, we propose defining the purpose of the company in the following way: the creation of economic and societal progress in a sustainable and wholly responsible way.[13]

In this context, the businessman or entrepreneur, individual or collective, would appear to be responsible for the meaning and purpose of economic progress.

This should be directed at the advancement of humanity and not to a logic of growth that has no other aim than itself.

It should not be subjected to a purely financial logic either.

Let us be aware of the danger that today represents the inconsiderate requirement of maximum shareholder profit and the dominant position occupied by financiers. These risk deflecting the company from its true function: that of real economic progress. In these circumstances, some might say, the company can no longer ensure the role of collective entrepreneur, its leaders no longer having enough space or autonomy to innovate, since they depend on a board dominated by shareholders. This is only partly true because the competition continues to come through, fundamentally due to innovation and technological advances. Moreover, the most enlightened leaders consider it their responsibility to convince shareholders and financiers that the long-term future of the company is better ensured by strategies of real economic progress than by financial stakes only.

Christian leaders and executives should therefore give meaning and direction, not only to their company, but also to the economic system within which they sit and which they lead.

Do they not have, furthermore, the responsibility to take a stand against abuses, surges and negative effects of a development model that by globalising, risks completely disassociating itself from politics and ethics?

Defining the *raison d'être* of the business firm in terms of economic progress will influence the strategies, the structures and the managerial behaviour of the firm as well as its specific contribution to the common good. It will pay greater attention to the societal consequences of his strategies and to the "externalities" of economic activity. This approach will also associate the entrepreneur-businessman with the collective responsibility of putting *science and technology* to the service of a true human development. In this perspective the Church doctrine on "Science and Faith" should be joined to its social doctrine to enlighten the economic decision taker.

A *raison d'être* of progress would allow the company to sit more clearly within the perspective of the Common Good. It could **direct its creative ability more towards the great challenges of our times**, such as climate and the environment, poverty and inequality, education and responsibility…This would facilitate a better use of the creativity of economic actors and their extraordinary entrepreneurial ability by putting them at the service of urgent planetary causes of the utmost importance. The project "Desertec" which aims to convert the desert sun into electricity is a spectacular move in this direction: it is led by a consortium of major German companies, government support and co-operation with the German branch of the Club of Rome… Solar power plants established in Africa could provide 15% of Europe's electricity needs by 2025.

Another Christian perspective for the business firm would be to orient its creative capacity toward the "bottom of the pyramid". Addressing the unsolvable needs and going to the encounter of the poorest, the business firm will not only help lift them from extreme poverty but could spark their own creativity and entrepreneurship and contribute to launch a dynamic of development. Some examples are already visible and convincing: Grameen Bank and micro-banking, the Transformational Business Network,[14] Danone Communities, Essilor and Aravind in India.[15]

Christian business leaders should test a new and strong assumption: an enterprise that is experiencing the encounter with the poor, the handicapped, the fragile, the excluded, can itself be transformed in depth and change its *raison d'être*, its mindset and its corporate culture.[16] If this approach is realistic it would offer the best link between the Gospel and the entrepreneurial co-creation.

The movement of *corporate social responsibility* begins to move in this direction by announcing products and distribution methods more in tune with the protection of the environment and the reduction of social inequalities.

When companies declare themselves responsible and announce it publicly, should they be taken seriously? Are we faced with slogans, wishful thinking and window dressing or are we already facing an emerging reality and concrete actions?

Observation of the companies suggests to us that some of them are resolutely committed in this way and that a change is thus possible. But will they be numerous enough to reverse the unidimensional thinking and transform the system? It is too early to say but a groundswell has begun and Christian leaders could play an informed and strong role in it.

What the early research shows[17] is the appearance of a new type of company, bypassing the purely instrumental logic and more concerned than before with the problems of society.

---

[14] Griffiths, B. and Tan, K., *Fighting Poverty through Enterprise. The Case for Social Venture Capital*, Transformational Business Network, 2007.

[15] Fontanet, X, *Si on faisait confiance aux entrepreneurs*, Manitoba/Les Belles Lettres, 2010.

[16] Ivan le Mintier, Communication aux Bernardins, October 10, 2010; *Oblat de l'abbaye de Fleury et entrepreneur social*, in Renaissance de Fleury, April 2011. See also Le Pichon, X, *Aux racines de l'homme: de la mort à l'amour*, Presses de la Renaissance, 1997 and 2010; *Sens ou non-sens de la "Fragilité Humaine" dans la Société Européenne contemporaine*, Colloque au Parlement européen, October 21, 2011. Vanier, J, and Kristova, J, *Leur regard perce nos ombres*, Fayard, 2011.

[17] See notably de Woot, Ph., 2005 and 2009, *op. cit.* and GRLI, *Global Responsible Leadership Initiative*, Bruxelles, 2005.

Four basic features characterise these companies:

- they have raised their *raison d'être* to the level of sustainable development;
- they reflect this in their strategies, their policies and their practices;
- they have been developing a culture of responsibility for a while;
- they consider this development as a process, a collective project that they can only carry out effectively with the support of their staff, civil society and the approval of public authorities.

The first concrete achievements are beginning to be felt. Some of these are convincing. The CSR Europe database sets out more than six hundred "best practices" for its members.[18] For some of them, we are clearly beyond a simple discourse of public relations.

To confront the great challenges of our time, the Lisbon Group[19] proposed a policy of major contracts between companies, the Government and civil society.

These would be realised in a co-operative fashion rather than one of competition and would allow major international public interest initiatives to be launched, for example:

- basic requirements with a view to reducing inequalities: water for two billion people, housing for one and a half billion, energy for two billion;
- the protection of the planet and the implementation of sustainable development;
- education and culture with a view to reinforcing tolerance and dialogue between
- civilisations and "identities";
- new methods of co-operation and participation favouring the emergence of global governance. (see the Millennium objectives)

---

[18] CSR Europe, www.csreurope.org/toolbox.

[19] The Lisbon Group, *Limits to Competition*, The MIT Press, Cambridge, Mass., 1995. See also Petrella, R., *Le manifeste de l'eau, pour un combat mondial (The water manifesto, for a global fight)*, Labor, Paris, 1998.

It is one more way to direct the skills and resources of individual and collective entrepreneur or businessman by other means than those of the market alone.

A new type of businessman or entrepreneur starts to appear. They have the characteristics of the classic entrepreneur but their motivations and the purpose of the businesses that they create are different and guided more by human and societal values. This shows that entrepreneurship and the creative ability can be developed outside of unidimensional thinking, escaping the sole measure of profit and applying to social and humanitarian causes. Muhammad Yunus is the archetype of this but others are beginning to come forward a little all around like Ashoka, the Triodos bank or, since long ago, Max Havelaar.[20] This new method of economic action could affect our economic system by example and contagion. It is a source of inspiration for the transformation of our companies and it would be interesting that the movements of Christian leaders are systematically learning from them in order to rethink the purpose of the company and creative participation.

The emergence of a truly connected economy and *integral humanism* as called for by Benedict XVI, also depends on our ability to innovate and create from new.

As Paul Dembinski said in his very detailed analysis of *Caritas in veritate*[21], it is the fundamental requirement of this message ... but all this is still to invent, to experiment, to rediscover ... and it is for us to begin to act without waiting for others.

Here again, the entrepreneurial qualities of leaders will be decisive.

The first innovations of this kind begin to emerge in addition to the hope that through a virtuous circle, "normal" companies will be won over by the example of these still marginal micro finance

---

[20] See notably Darnil, S., and Leroux, M., *80 Hommes pour changer le monde (Men to change the world)*, J C Lattès, Paris, 2005. Cherisey, de, M.H. and L, *Passeurs d'espoir*, Paris, Presses de la Renaissance, 2005.

[21] Dembinski, P., *De l'incomplétude de l'économie, lecture économique et critique de l'encyclique "Caritas in veritate" de Benoît XVI (Of the incompleteness of the economy, economic reading and critique of the encyclical "Caritas in veritate" of Benedict XVI*, L'AGEFI, August 10, 2009.

practices, of the united economy or the economy of communion in which giving and generosity play a central role.

Such an approach would allow us to *loosen* the stifling constraints of unidimentional thinking and of instrumental logic.

2-2 LEADERSHIP AND ETHICS

Leadership

Management is no longer enough. If one is to put ethics back at the heart of economic activity, we need leaders and not only managers or administrators.

As we have seen, one of the roles of the leader is to develop entrepreneurship and the organisation's creativity. Another role is to lead it as a human reality, to motivate its staff and to undertake cultural change for a more ethical and sustainable development.

In order to do this do we not need a new type of leader nowadays?

The idea of leaders capable of driving a changing society is as old as the world.

Companies were mostly in "deadlock" because their leaders were locked in an outdated ideology and didn't know how to adapt.

> Empty heads bearing the weight of great legacies and worn out hearts dragging themselves after dignities that resemble them. *(Lacordaire)*

At the end of the Old Regime, the Prince de Ligne wrote to an ambitious young man who asked for his advice: *Be only mediocre and you will go far.* (Current translation: *Do not depart from unidimensional thinking and you will go far*). He understood the inertia of structures and methods of recruitment. His elegant verve denounced the danger that threatens all changing societies: the co-option of the same by the same.

Are we not too often locked in our limited belief in the virtues of a purely instrumental economic model?

> Sire, if one considers where the good minds have led France, it might be worth trying the bad ones. *(Mirabeau to Louis XVI)*

Vast research has shown that the best performing companies are those whose leaders succeed in establishing a sufficient balance between their professional skills as managers and their personal qualities as leaders.

While Frederik Taylor recommended *replacing the government of men by the administration of things*, quite the opposite should be done. It consists today in rebalancing the economy, on the one hand with ethics, and politics on the other.

If one narrowly defines *management*, one might say that it consists above all in the administration of things: objectives, budgets, strategic analyses, plans, methods, procedures… *Leadership* is the art of directing the human reality: it is the motivation, the communication, the participation, and the ability to convince people of the values that one wishes to implement. It rests on moral authority and it is through it that ethics are passed down into the company.

Everybody knows the necessity and usefulness of management and its *methods*.

When the first man landed on the moon, the director of NASA pleased himself with a very sober statement: *The power of the method! This method has enabled ordinary men to do something extraordinary.* And these people were four hundred thousand, twenty thousand companies and two hundred universities. Who would not believe that this is an approach of considerable power? As we have previously suggested for creativity, should we not put this extraordinary management skill at the service of the great global combats that we will have to lead if we are to confront the challenges of the climate and of poverty?

When these methods are participatory, they facilitate teamwork.

When they become more technical than participatory they risk disassociating the management of the company from its human and political reality. They become mere instruments of maximisation without regard for what can not be easily measured such as, for example, creativity, motivation, support for a collective project and its purposes. When leaders are merely technicians of performance and profitability, they often become incapable of ethics and politics.

It must be recognised that the dominant culture is still that of all-too exclusively technical *management*.

And here, **the role of business schools** is crucial.

These could become important agents of cultural change if they were willing to transform and rise up to the level of challenges facing us. But their assurance, if not their arrogance, makes one doubt their will to fundamentally question themselves: "the way in which we teach is by far the best in training for management and leadership," unflinchingly declares the Dean of an important business school.[22]

The *raison d'être* of most of these schools is to equip their students to run the existing system in an ever more effective way without asking questions about its aims, its faults or the dangers it poses. In this way, the majority of professors are the thurifers of an ideology, the clergy and the celebrants of a unidimensional way of thinking. They claim to train citizens and yet they more often train mere robots of a system without a clear *raison d'être*. They constitute a major obstacle to the establishment of a culture of sustainable development. This is also true for most universities or schools of Christian tradition.

A radical change in these schools is necessary but it will only occur if the universities of which they are members are willing to commit to it themselves.

Without responsible leadership at all levels, companies risk not taking good care of their staff, which then becomes a mere "resource", a "cost" rather than a precious investment. Alienation, exploitation, demotivation, permanent redundancies and all the suffering of men and women follow on from this.

> Why must it be that our businesses, of which nothing should justify but economic creativity, often be so destructive of humanity?[23]

Today, we have enough managers, technicians and financiers. What is lacking for a change in culture to happen, is an adequate number of leaders and executives capable of conceiving and bringing about a thorough transformation by inspiring those who must implement it, and also capable of creating a social legitimacy that is beginning to sorely lack in certain companies.

---

[22] Business Education, *Financial Times Supplement*, April 28, 2003.
[23] Grenet, X., *Cahiers d'un DRH (DRH Workbooks)*, Cerf, Paris, 2008.

This is where the role of leader becomes important.

It is in **the exercise of power** that leaders most clearly show their ethical commitment or their indifference.

Focusing on leadership requires some caution because it relies in part on the talents, character and the intuition. It carries with it the temptation of excessive self-reliance, of an ambition that is more personal than collective, of a neglect of rigorous, demanding and professional approaches without flair.

All those involved in action know that great leaders owe a part of their authority to their personal qualities. It is a constant fact of human history.

Baudelaire suggested a good definition of talent when he asked his friends: *Have you ever wondered about what was in you that was not acquired through education, or work, or money?* What, if not the gifts of the fairies that looked over our cradle, the charismas, the graces received, this part of us that is innate? It can be developed and enhanced but, initially, it consists in a gift over which we have little control.

This is therefore an essential ingredient of leadership. But it is a dangerous ingredient because it can also compromise the collective gameplay necessary for the performance of the company. If we attach too much importance to talents, personality, individual dynamism, we risk casting aside from the game those who should normally participate in it, even if they are less talented. The temptation to centralise and personalise power too much becomes great. A joke will illustrate this point. A leader to whom I asked what amused him the most in his job answered: *It is the unsolved problems, those on which all of my colleagues break their teeth . . . ; for then they need the Holy Spirit and they call me.*

The Gospel tells us that we must build on those talents and put them to good use in the values that we are defending and the establishment of the Kingdom. This is why the leadership that we pin all our hopes on is the carrier of values of humanisation and of the Common Good. It must be the bearer of the ethical and political dimensions that our economic model is so lacking. And we know fully well that this is not always the case.

The business leaders do not like us speaking about their power. When we broach the subject, they modestly lower their eyes, they evoke the concepts of leadership, management, supervision . . . But the stark reality of power – that of ambition, conquest, intrigue, *raison d'état* – we do not reveal it. It is as though we are dealing with an inappropriate, lewd and dangerous subject. Men do not discuss their passions. And yet...

> I place at the forefront, as a general inclination of all of mankind, a perpetual and relentless desire to acquire power after power. *(Hobbes)*

> This appetite for domination, amongst all human passions, is the most exhilarating... *(Saint Augustine)*

> Despite what the hypocritical ministers say, power is the first of all pleasures. *(Stendhal)*

The issue is critical. It consists of the age-old problem of good or bad government: government of people and countries, or simply governments of the most diverse organisations.

It is a great thing to have power over others... (Guichardin)

Like a distant echo, this wisdom still speaks to all those who exercise or suffer power. It speaks softly in organisations that weave our democracies and our economy; in violent cries where the arbitrary, violence and injustice reign.

There are two conceptions of power. One is cynical, cold, calculating, amoral: it is the power of *domination*. The other is humanistic, democratic, imbued with ethical values: it is the power of *service*.[24]

The power of domination arises from the belief that the world is a jungle and that men are bad or lazy. It is thus necessary to use coercion and deception and only to follow moral rules when they coincide with the interests of the organisation or the *raison d'état*.

The power of service acts as if the world could be humanised and man was perfectible. It is by the laws and justice, ethics and compassion, that we will establish co-operation and collective efficiency.

---

[24] de Woot, Ph., *Méditation sur le pouvoir (Contemplation of power)*, De Boeck et Larcier, 1998.

Any person in a situation of power is almost always crossed by these two opposing logics. The consistent choice with Christian values is obviously to uphold the power of service, the first type of power often making man regress, the second, on the contrary, helping him to progress.

> The Son of Man has come to serve. *(John)*
>
> ... [and he] began to wash his disciples' feet, drying them with the towel that was wrapped around him.
>
> ..., do you understand what I have done for you? he asked them.
>
> Now that I, your Lord and Teacher, have washed your feet, you also should wash one another's feet. I have set you an example that you should do as I have done for you. *(John 13:4–5, 12–15)*

The two conceptions of power inspire very different behaviour.

The results of research in this field show, in a simplified way, that the method of exercising power is linked to a set of attitudes that determine the climate and human culture of the company. This is not the place to describe them in detail but recourse to "classic" pearls of wisdom will undoubtedly make them felt in a concrete manner, even if it is a little (barely) of a caricature. The conciseness of the maxims will preserve the depth and will lead us back to basics. Their subtlety or their malice will prevent us from falling into the spirit of the system and will force us to stay on track.

The behaviours of **domination** are linked to the following traits

- A strong personalisation of power
  He wanted to rule by himself, this jealousy became his weakness. (Saint Simon about Louis XIV)

- Ambitions and strong appetites
  Their ambition is like the horizon that has always gone before them. (Montesquieu)
  If I were offered the place of God the Father, I would refuse it. It is a stalemate. (Napoleon)

- Secrecy and mistrust
  Courtier's friendship, faith of foxes and government of wolves.
  (La Bruyère)
  The permanent conspiracy is the true nature of power. (Balzac)

- Lack of listening
  Nothing important happens to other people. (Saying of a Minister of
  Louis XV)

- A sense of personal superiority
  Often wrong, never in doubt! (Mirabeau)
  And we must count them for a lot every time that they count
  themselves for everything. (Retz)

- Indifference and sometimes contempt for people
  ...the King's subjects and livestock... (Chronicle of the XVIIth
  century)

- A certain vanity or *certain* vanity
  They walk like monkeys beneath the purple and donkeys under
  beneath the lion's skin. (Erasmus)

- An atmosphere of court and courtesans.
  The praise, or rather, the flattery, pleased him so much so that even
  the coarsest were well received, the lowest even better appreciated.
  (Saint Simon about Louis XIV)

The behaviours of **service** are linked to all other traits

- Participation and support
  I want nothing of that which puts a role in the place of a man.
  (Chamfort)

- A sense of common purpose
  Do not forget where the path leads. (Heraclitus)

- Trust and transparency
  We must remove the masks from both things and people. (Montaigne)

> *The truth sheds, when it has a certain carat, a brilliance which we cannot resist. (Retz)*

- Listening and communication
  The word half belongs to he who speaks it, and half to he who hears it. (Montaigne)

- The organisation of collective gameplay
  For the essential, unity.
  For the contingent, freedom.
  For all, communion. (Saint Augustine)

- Respect for and knowledge of people
  To respect a man, is to be kept awake by his mystery. (Levinas)

- A degree of humility and humour
  If you do not feel able to get over the prestige of ruling, renounce the power, you are not worthy of it; put yourself to work in the fields. (Pythagoras)

- An atmosphere of freedom
  I equally hate the clown and the inflated ego: you would not be friends with one nor the other. (Pascal)

The stakes are high.

Depending of your method of exercising power, the atmosphere within the company will be very different as well as the opportunities for participation and personal development. The creative support or the apprehensive recesses will inspire behaviour.

Ultimately, the difference will be that of alienation or empowerment.

> It is an eternal experience that every man who has power is led to abuse it *(Montesquieu)*

> Woe to the worthless shepherd, who deserts the flock! *(Zachariah 11:17)*

Ethics and the responsible leader

In meaning to be responsible, leaders and companies thereby commit to an ethical approach.

Who mentions responsibility means answering for one's actions and their consistency in relation to a system of values that relates to a conception of man, of society and of the future.

If the company wants to give meaning to its activities, if it wants to give sense to economic progress by inserting it into other forms of human progress, the ethical dimension is essential to inform its choices and to guide its behaviour.

For a Christian business leader, the central and challenging question is the following: is it possible in one's professional life to live according to the values of the Gospel and to conduct oneself in an ethical manner by leading a system that is not?

From the outset, let us remember that ethics is not confined to integrity. But of course, it is important. We know that the market economy is based on the trust and respect for the rules of the game. If these elements disappear, the system may disintegrate. It consists here in the essential honesty that ensures compliance with standards: truth, visibility, mutual trust. But this is not enough.

Often however, this basic level of ethics is not practised.

In a competitive and complex world, the choice is very rarely black and white and is most often in shades of grey. It is there that blunders are common and that the performance of the company may outweigh all other considerations.

The mild form of this is "be competitive without lying too much, without cheating too much, without stealing too much". Are you offended? Think about fiscal engineering, advertising exaggerations, expense accounts, "sweeteners" to convince the buyer...

The virulent forms are those of "salus firmae suprema lex" where all means are permitted if the company is in peril or, even worse, immoral pressures to achieve unreasonable profits and to take unnecessary risks by playing on the greed of the players and the naivety of customers. The current crisis provides numerous illustrations.

> Woe to you, teachers of the law and Pharisees, you hypocrites! You give a tenth of your spices – mint, dill and cumin. But you have neglected

the more important matters of the law – justice, mercy and faithfulness. You should have practised the latter, without neglecting the former. You blind guides! *(Matthew 23:23–26)*

But the real ethical question of our time is at another level than that of the integrity alone. It is that of knowing *what world we want to build together with the vast resources and the enormous skills at our disposal.*

In an irreversible time, men are historical beings and their actions build the world. They are responsible for the future and the society that they are in the process of creating.

> In the daily commitment, it depends on us – in a very limited but real way – that history shapes or does not shape the Kingdom. There where we are, it is our responsibility that life enlightens or darkens, that there is more happiness or suffering: we are accountable to others and before God, for our very limited and narrow circle, and within the limits of our freedom.[25]

This responsibility is all the more so for the leaders as their creativity and power are more important. As we have seen, this is the case of the company and the economic system that it leads.

Refusing to integrate ethics into the direction and operations of the company and the market under the pretext that the economy has its own logic, comes to lock itself in an instrumental approach (unidimensional thinking) and deprives the company and the market of their social legitimacy. If they are trapped too much in a logic of means, do some leaders, like honest men, not risk illustrating the realistic description of Peggy: *the world is full of honest people, we recognise them because they make bad moves with awkwardness?*[26]

Convictions and responsibility

In the ethical domain it is **our values, our moral convictions** that establish the difference between what we perceive as *good* and what we perceive as *bad* or, more subtly, between the *best* and the *worst*.

---

[25] Berten, I., *Croire en un Dieu trinitaire (Belief in a trinitary God)*, Fidélité, 2008.
[26] Péguy, Ch., *Clio*, Gallimard, Paris, 1917.

They are a matter of conscience and they enlighten our choices and our behaviours.

In a globalising world, the question of knowing what type of company we want to build should be based on values that are as universal as possible.

Is this realistic in a world torn between hurtling modernity, unidimensional thinking, individualism, on the one hand and on the other hand, tradition, the refusal of modern development and fundamentalism? Is this possible in a world where "murderous identities" develop more than ever?[27]

Is this even possible in the West in a pluralistic society that has moved away from religious beliefs and that would like to eliminate all previous constraints, all restrictions on liberty, creativity and personal expression even if that is lacking in content and meaning. Is this possible in a society tempted by relativism and the denial of collective values? Frenzied *"all ego"* individualism is probably not the noble pathway for a universal morale.

This, however, finds a primary embodiment in the Universal Declaration of Human Rights.

> Its proclamation is certainly a historical fact of vital importance that gives concrete expression, albeit partial, to the humanism of our time. But this expression must be considered as being only an approximation of an inspiring vision, in which we are able to discern the manifestation of the ethical dimension of man... [28]

It falls to Christian business leaders to vigorously defend these rights and to give them some specificity. This is largely what the social doctrine of the Church does. It is *the affirmation of fundamental principles from which the necessary changes are thought out, by drawing on strategies or the societal goals towards which one must strive.*[29]

---

[27] Maalouf, A., *Les identités meurtrières (Deadly identities)*, Grasset, Paris, 1998.

[28] Ladrière, J., *L'humanisme contemporain (Contemporary humanism)*, in Quid, Revista de Filosofia, Numero: Sobre a experiencia, Lisboa, Livros Cotovia? 2001, pp. 445–465.

[29] Berten, I., *L'enseignement social de l'Eglise: bilan et perspectives (The social teaching of the Church: balance and perspectives)*, in Berten, Buekens and Martinez, Enterrée, la doctrine sociale? (Is social doctrine buries?) Bruxelles, Lumen Vitae, 2009, pp. 15–37.

But ethics are not limited to convictions or values. They focus primarily on our actions and their consequences. It is in action that ethics are embodied, in this way, it involves a commitment. It is here that it becomes real and that leadership finds its true dimension.

The ethic of responsibility requires that one commit oneself, that one chooses a direction, that one decides to transform fate into destiny.

It consists in a permanent *critical commitment*[30] so as not to become the "pebble tossed around by the waves". It consists in a constant reply to the unacceptable..

This *must be expressed and consolidated each day.*
Each time a Creon appears, an Antigone must return.[31]

Guided by values, the ethic of responsibility takes account not only of behaviours themselves but also the consequences of our decisions and our actions. Intentions are not enough. One must take responsibility for the fallout of the action. The popular proverb saying that *the road to hell is paved with good intentions* clearly reflects ethical insufficiency of an action, or an inaction, of which one would not assume the consequences.

Ethics begin at the first cry of human suffering, at the point where one finds oneself facing another person. It prevents us from being indifferent to the suffering of others, *a fortiori* if we ourselves have caused it.[32]

In a positive way, we can define ethics as *a process of life that is always searching for the solution that will bring the most love.*[33]

Our economic and technological system gradually substituted the world of reason for one of emotion and conscience: the world of things in the world of humans.

The world of reason is governed by the natural laws that intelligence uncovers and to which it is submitted. It is that which

---

[30] de Stexhe, G., *Cours d'éthique (Ethics) 2007*, Facultés Universitaires Saint Louis, Bruxelles.

[31] Lambert, D., *Sciences et théologie (Science and theology)*, Lessius, Bruxelles, 1999.

[32] See Fourez, C., *La construction des sciences. Introduction à la philosophie et à l'éthique des sciences (The construction of science: Introduction to the philosophy and the ethics of science)*, De Boeck, 1988.

[33] Cochinaux, Ph., *L'éthique (Ethics)*, Fidélité, 2007.

leads science and its applications, technology and production; it is that which presides over the organisation of the society regulated by law; it is that which tries to replace the arbitrary and violence with the rule of law and the market.

The world of man as a subject is part of the conscience, emotion and free will; it is *the effort of the person to build himself as an individual and not be subject to instrumental logic*[34]; it is one's own anxious conscience, the questioning of meaning, the call for personal freedom and responsibility; it is the world of emotions, heart, soul, love, religion, gratitude for one another; it is also the world of doubt and questioning.

A widening gap is developing between the objective world of reason and the subjective world of conscience, between the "hot" world of humans and the "cold" world of objects manipulated by techniques. The danger augments with a total disassociation of the system from its actors, of tools from purpose, of means from ends. Such a system becomes immoral if its operation has only its own efficiency and survival for rules. As such, the question once more arises of knowing what the prognosis of ethics is in a purely instrumental system? What response can Christian leaders bring about?

Love thy neighbour

For leaders and executives, the closest neighbour is obviously the staff of the company and to which may be added stakeholders such as the suppliers, the customers, the region, etc... This is where the testimony of Christian leaders seems to be the most prevalent and convincing.[35]

Choosing human dignity as a central value makes a fundamental difference to the atmosphere, participation and personal development. Current competitive pressures threaten this kind of approach but it is essential to keep it. The social doctrine of the Church is clear in this regard.

---

[34] Touraine, A., *La critique de la modernité (The critic of modernity)*, Fayard, 1992.

[35] See notably, for France, Audoyer, J.P., *Patrons et chrétiens (Patrons and Christians)*, Editions de l'Emmanuel, 2002.

Salaries, working conditions and health are essential elements, but the key to dignity at work is the degree of responsibility that the company confers on its workers.

The encyclical *Mater and Magistra* is perfectly clear on this point.

> If the structures and operations of an economic system are of a nature to compromise the human dignity of those who work under them, to blunt their sense of responsibility, to take every personal initiative away from them, then we consider this system unjust, even if the wealth produced reaches a high level and is distributed according to the laws of justice and equity.[36]

The real challenge is to give work back the meaning of its participation in the collective project of the company by increasing its creativity (*ergon*) and by reducing its monotony or its drudgery (*ponos*).[37]

It is important to implement in a concrete manner what we learn from modern anthropology. Man does not work in the company solely as "homo economicus". He goes there with all of his aspirations: material (to live, to have an income, security...); symbolic (recognition, power to act, to influence, to be informed...); spiritual (belonging to a meaningful community, sharing life experiences, solidarity, fraternity...).[38]

An impressive example of this sort of human progress is that of the Ouimet companies in Canada. It shows that such human progress is possible and compatible with the pressures of a competitive economy.[39] It is one of the very rare systematic steps to soundly implement the social doctrine of the Church by going far beyond mere discussions or generous intentions. *The business plan outlines the human, moral, economic, social, spiritual and religious responsibilities of the company and its staff... It seeks to reconcile the well-being of men and*

---

[36] Jean XXIII, *Encyclique Mater et Magistra*, Spes, 1962.

[37] Buttet, N., *le Travail (Work)*, Conférence au séminaire d'été d'Ecophilos, Fribourg, August 2008.

[38] Arnsperger, Ch., *op. cit.*

[39] Ouimet, J.-R., *Entretiens avec Yves Semen. 'Tout vous a été confié' (Interviews with Yves Semen, "All has been entrusted to you")*, Paris, Presses de la Renaissance, 2008.

woman in the workplace with the demands of profitability, which are imperative to the survival and development of every business. This company has developed an integrated system of management tools (ISMT) as much in the human domain as in the economic domain. This dual approach is based on the belief that *the combined action of these activities was likely to generate lasting values that contribute to the development of people in their workplace...values of humanisation contributing to the development of each person individually and in his relationships with others... values of spiritualisation contributing to the fulfilment of each person in his desire to unify his life and give it meaning.* The step is managed very professionally, but also very openly and respectfully of the freedom of everyone. It is based on concrete practices and actions sufficiently organised to become a true business culture. Evaluation tools have been implemented to ensure that the company stays on track and has the ability to promote lasting coherence between the development of people and economic performance.

Who is my neighbour today?

After the next nearest, should the responsibility of economic actors not be extended to the dimensions of the system itself and to question the negative aspects and the consequences of globalisation and its failings? If the central values are those of human dignity and the survival of the planet, should the leaders and executives not feel more responsible for the system that they lead and for its consequences for those that it alienates, dismisses, demodes and for those for whom it destroys the traditional structures.

If ethics begin at the first cry of human suffering, should we not listen to the clamour of those that our development model, our instrumental logic, our unidimensional thinking make suffer in one way or another? Listen to them directly whenever possible or to their spokespersons as they start to multiply.

Perhaps one of the first stages of a truly ethical step would be to emerge from a state of indifference to one which does not directly fall under instrumental efficiency, and to listen to the cries of those who suffer at the hands of our economic system.

Indifference makes us deaf and blind. It is a denial of man.

We played the flute for you, and you did not dance;
We sang a dirge, and you did not cry. *(Luke 7:32)*

He saw him and he passed away. *(Luke 7:31)*

All of the Gospel shows us that Jesus makes a fundamental choice: he puts himself in the shoes of the poor and the sinner, that is to say all those who are marginalised from polite society and the religion in place...This choice is an attitude of the heart, an insight and a practice.

Attitude of the heart, that is to say the fact of letting oneself be touched by the situation, the cry, the suffering face of another. Insight: it is the deliberate choice to look at situations and events from those who are not beneficiaries. In practice: it is there, where we stand, take party for the suffering by opening up to him the possibilities of life, dignity and happiness.[40]

Giving meaning to entrepreneurship and creativity

Is a major ethical task for Christian leaders and executives not, as I suggested above, giving sense to the specific function of the company and replying solidly to the following questions: *economic and technical progress for what? for whom? how?*

These questions are of an ethical and political nature. The market alone is unable to answer them.

Why? Must it really be that our economic empowerment and our extraordinary creative ability consecrate so much effort and resources to the development of ever more profitable markets and a society of frenzied consumerism and be constantly revitalised by feverish, intrusive and often crude advertising? Are there not prior needs in the world that are unsatisfied and whose importance is incommensurate with the progresses of hyper-comfort or pleasures worthy of Roman decadence?

---

[40] Berten, I., *op.cit.*

For whom? Is it morally acceptable and politically reasonable to tolerate half of mankind being excluded from the benefits of creativity and the dynamism of an economy that functions without or against it? Will we tolerate for much longer the paradox of unprecedented creation of wealth in human history and poverty affecting several billions of people?

How? Will the race for growth that rich countries are involved in become increasingly independent of the utmost problems of the planet? Will it continue for much longer to pollute the atmosphere, to exhaust limited resources, to promote a kind of individualistic society, trapped in the bubble of its successes and its privileges?

Let us repeat: in a global economy, the *raison d'être* of the company is to achieve economic and technical progress in the perspective of true human progress and of a democratic debate on the type of world that we would like to construct together.

Do the Christian leaders and executives adequately embody the necessary transformation of our economic system and do they proclaim highly enough the invitation of Jesus to take care of the weakest and the poorest and to henceforth realise the Kingdom?

> Do not wait... to start giving the poor their place: here and now the shape of the world can start to change, here and now the Kingdom of God can begin to happen ... Now is the time to make room for the poor and to open to all freedom, so that everyone has his place in society, that everyone has the right to integration and to participation.[41]

Ethic of foresight

We must go further still and assume, as much as possible, the responsibility for the future that we are preparing for ourselves. According to Bergson, *consciousness is a bridge between that which has been and that which will be, a bridge between the past and the future.*[42]

---

[41] Berten, I., *op.cit.*

[42] Bergson, H., *Les deux sources de la morale et de la religion (The two sources of morality and religion)*, Presses universitaires de France, 1932.

This obviously concerns the planet. This also concerns new and difficult issues posed by constant scientific discoveries.

Hans Jonas[43] proposed a very interesting train of thought on this subject. He argues that new dimensions of human activity and *monstrous technical progress* and its power over man call for an ethic of foresight and responsibility that is a match for these challenges. He recalls *the sacrosanct nature of man* and warns against the scientific and technical developments that could affect it.

He adds to it *safeguarding the planet* as a condition of human survival.

This approach gave rise to the principle of precaution. That which often annoys leaders, probably wrongly because the caution with regard to the future is symbolised in history by Cassandra. Everyone laughed at her, but she was right: Troy was taken, burned and transformed into fields of rubble.

> It is still the same band of these that flouted Cassandra in Troy and Jeremiah in Jerusalem.[44]

This responsibility for the future must remind us that we are engaged in a cosmic history. Science has shown that the cosmos had a beginning and developed over time, that there was a *flèche du temps* (time as an arrow) and that time was irreversible (Lemaître, Prigogine...).

It has also shown us that life progressed in the direction of a growing *complexity-awareness* (Darwin, Teilhard de Chardin, de Duve).

History tells us of many attempts by men to become more civilised and humanised. There is thus a story of the cosmos, a story of life, a story of men. For Christians, there is also a story of salvation which is to happen when the *Kingdom of God will reunite all its scattered children.*

The continuation of the creation towards greater humanity, greater union and communion should thus guide our ethical approach and our political commitment.

---

[43] Jonas, H., *Le principe responsabilité (The main responsibility)*, Flammarion, 2000.
[44] Zweig, S., *op. cit.*

In this historical perspective, our choices are not just individual, they are also collective. They become so more and more because of globalisation and growing interdependence. It is here that ethics rejoins politics, as we shall see in the following section.

Companies will be forced to use their creative ability to innovate in the social domain and to prepare for the advent of a more humane economy. Organisations of Christian leaders and executives could systematically gather innovations of this type to disseminate them, discuss them and to spur on the changes of which they are the bringers.

An ethical culture

In a complex world we have seen that ethics are never simple. It rarely boils down to black and white evidence, or good or bad. It arises mostly in terms of better or worse, and shades of grey. It does not boil down to the enunciation of a code of conduct promulgated by management and "faithfully" applied by staff.

It is the entire corporate culture that must change if it wishes to become responsible and to transform its behaviour. It is the reason why Corporate Social Responsibility (CSR) movements will only really influence change if they agree to base their approach on a deeper understanding of ethics and the cultural evolution than it implies. These exchanges of "good practices" will only be useful if they base themselves on solid concepts and values to move beyond the stage of tools and instruments.

In terms of ethics, cultural evolution involves developing it as a basic thinking that permeates all levels of the company and each of its functions: finance, marketing, research, etc... To do this, one can create in the company *an ethical space* where this cultural process should become visible, active, continuous and could face *the inexhaustible complexity of reality.*[45] Such a space would be the place where these new attitudes would be developed; a place of interrogation, alertness, anxiety, listening; a place where the desire to understand other views would prevail over the temptation to

---

[45] Maesschalk, M., L'éthique entre formalisme et subjectivité, *in L'éthique des affaires* (The ethics between formalism and subjectivity, in *Business ethics*), Louvain la Neuve, Ciaco, 1995.

condemn what one perceives as hostile or simply critical, as in NGOs for example.

A place where one would accept questioning, where one would refine the ethical judgement by comparing what is desirable and what is possible, the greater good and the lesser evil, the values and the realities? A place where one would distinguish between *the best and the worst, between the extraordinary and the impossible (Retz)*. A place where one would only accept the necessary compromises in full awareness, by using a more cautious response to the challenges and contradictions that beset us. A place that would fire up particularly in ethical moments.

> "Ethical moments" are most often referred to in situations where the future conduct is all but clearly defined, because the aims are not clear, or even multiple and at least partially contradictory; where the relationship between the aims and the systems of means are also far from being unequivocal, and where generalisation is impossible, because no concrete situation is thoroughly identical to another.[46]

The existence of an ethical space in the company would help executives and leaders to discover a true freedom that they are so often denied by a system that does not leave them any room for manoeuvre.

Such ethical spaces are beginning to appear. This is notably the case of the *Nanoscience Centre* in Cambridge.[47] Its 120 researchers want to avoid the errors of GMOs. Open debates are undertaken from the outset of the research before too greatly divided or polarised positions emerge. They believe that we cannot leave unanswered the fundamental questions that affect values, choices for the future and interests involved in the conduct of such research.

At the level of the economic system as a whole such spaces should be multiplied. Some professional associations are beginning to do so. As for employers' associations, they do not really play this role. They

---

[46] Cobbaut, R., *Ethique et régulation des système financiers (Ethics and regulation of financial systems)*, in Cours d'éthique des affaires et finalité de l'entreprise, IAG, Université de Louvain, Louvain la Neuve, 1997.

[47] Wilsdon, J., *Nanotech needs to listen to its public and now, FT*, September 1, 2004.

should expand their mission that is still too often limited to the defence of the interests of their members and forces them to place themselves at the level of lowest common denominator. Other groups are in the process of forming themselves around the concept of sustainable development and the societal responsibilities of the company. They could become ethical spaces like the ones we are talking about.

In Europe, associations of Christian leaders and young employers have played this role for a long time but do they still do so adequately? Is their voice prophetic enough, are their efforts sufficiently numerous and audacious to contribute to the development of the system and to replace unidimensional thinking with an ethic worthy of this name?

2-3 STATESMANSHIP AND COMMON GOOD

It is a requirement of justice and charity to want the Common Good.[48]

There is a new obligation which is not only ethical but also political. Economic globalisation advances much faster than *global governance*. It escapes nation states and gradually imposes its logic on the whole world. This backwardness of politics with respect to economics leads to a kind of public helplessness to drive real development strategies and to democratically debate the societal issues of globalisation. As Raymond Aron has said, the nation states have become too small for big problems and too big for small ones. If there is often over-regulation at the national level, there is virtually no economic regulation at the global level.

Should business leaders not participate more actively in the research and definition of the Common Good of our time and try to build it into their sphere of activity even if global governance is still in its infancy? Should they not play a more responsible role in the emergence of a new culture of co-operation and debate that would replace the simple current "lobbying"?

---

[48] Benedict XVI, *Caritas in veritate*, 7, 2009.

To their role of *entrepreneur* and *leader* should they not add that of *statesman* in the construction of new governance and adopt a role of concerned citizens?

> Humanity is a reality to be built, it is a task, it is ahead of us.[49]

On this point, the social doctrine of the Church is clear, but do enough Christian leaders listen to it? Are they the seeds of a "political" commitment of the company in favour of a large societal dialogue in view of deeply transforming our economic system? Could Christian leaders and executives exercise a globalising economic power without placing it more actively within the perspective of a Common Good that becomes that of the whole planet?[50]

What common good? Babel or Pentecost?

The biblical story of **Babel** describes the temptation of unlimited material development, enclosed in a dominant or totalitarian ideology.

> We build ourselves a town and a tower whose highest point is in the heavens...[51]:

Prometheus unchained, purposeless capitalism, morrows that sing ("power to the Soviets and the electrification of Siberia"), scientism and positivism...

> Let us make a name for ourselves in order not to be dispersed on the surface of the ground...:

Unidimensional model, withdrawal behind our own ethical or cultural identity, closure, logic of power, "centre of the world without

---

[49] Ladrière, J., *La conception chrétienne de l'homme (the Christian conception of man)*, Conférence de Budapest, 1985.

[50] See notably Delcourt, J., and de Woot, Ph. (Ed.), *Babel ou Pentecôte: les défis de la globalisation (Babel or Pentecost: the challenges of globalisation)*, Louvain la Neuve, Presses Universitaires de l'UCL, 1994.

[51] *Genèse, 11*, Bible, Osty, Seuil, 1973.

asking any question neither about others nor about humanity in general"[52] ...

The whole of the earth had one language, the same words ... :

Refusal of diversity, debate, criticism and questioning, dominant ideology.
Instrumental logic, conformity to the ideology of the market ...

Nothing from now on will be unachievable from what they decide to do ... :

Seemingly limitless power of economic action without clear *raison d'être* and served by the extraordinary creativity of the techno-sciences.
Pentecost offers a different message. It speaks of openness, plurality, dialogue and listening to one another.

[They] began to speak in other tongues, each one heard them speaking in his own language [as the Spirit had enabled them] ...
Utterly amazed, they asked: how is it that each of us hears them in his own native language?
Some, however, made fun of them and said, "they have had too much sweet wine". *(Apostles 2:4–13)*

What world do we want to build?
A world dominated by a frenzied technological race and market fundamentalism, a world in the process of pollution and destruction; a world of inequalities, social injustices, emigrations, exclusion and alienation; a world where systems often overwhelm actors, where individual egos, both regional and national, outweigh the solidarity needed; a world of deadly competition, where consumerism is everywhere, both short term and channel hopping; a world of cheap publicity and seclusion; a world so unequal that it breeds violence and terror ...

---

[52] Bottéro, J., *Au commencement étaient les dieux (At the beginning were the gods)*, Hachette, 2004.

Or do we actually want to contribute to the advent of a fairer and more united world?

Are we ready to fight to transform our economic system into a model of sustainable development, to change our ways of living to preserve the earth and better share out resources, to "manage the earth like a garden"? Will we let instrumental thinking guide our economic decisions or will we try to focus more and more effort on the creation of human progress? Do we want to construct a world that is more welcoming, warmer, and more tolerant, *a world where people can be human together?*[53]

> Building between men, across all borders, a new kind of solidarity – universal, complex, subtle, thoughtful, and adult – a solidarity that can transcend nations, communities, ethnic groups, without abolishing the proliferation of cultures.[54]

Is that not Pentecost?

> Is this not the kind of fasting I have chosen:
> to loosen the chains of injustice
> and untie the cords of the yoke,
> to set the oppressed free
> and break every yoke?
> Is it not to share your food with the hungry
> and to provide the poor wanderer with shelter –
> when you see the naked, to clothe him...
> Then your light will break forth like the dawn... *(Isaiah 58:6–8)*

What world do we want to bring forth?

Favoured by globalisation, the market ideology, now of uniform thinking, is gaining global ground. The "victory" of capitalism over communism reinforced business leaders and financiers in their feeling of legitimacy and in their belief in an

---

[53] Vanier, J., *Car c'est de l'homme qu'il s'agit (For it relates to man)*, Rencontres de St Nicolas et Dorothée de Flüe, St Maurice, November, 2008.

[54] Maalouf, A., *Le dérèglement du monde (The deregulation of the world)*, Paris, Grasset, 2009.

automatic liaison between the dynamism of the market economy and the progress of humanity. Their model would successfully impose itself on the whole world and promised more credible "bright futures" than those of directed economic systems. Thanks to its gradual globalisation and its growing power over technical, financial and managerial resources, this model prevailingly controls the main key points of the global economy. In this position, the actors that lead it significantly influence the political orientations of the planet and tend to make prevalent without sufficient debate, not only their model of development, but also the ideology that underlies it. Is this acceptable from a democratic point of view?

Can the "global" Common Good be defined and maintained by the market economy alone with no other aim than its own efficiency?

The social doctrine of the Church is well developed in this domain.[55] It formulates its vision of the fundamental and inalienable rights of the person, based on a model of development that provides social welfare over time, on Peace, security and support – or the advent – of a just order. It also speaks of subsidiarity, responsibility and solidarity.

The Church defines the Common Good as *the set of social conditions that allow all people and all groups that make up society to achieve their own accomplishments in the most positive manner.*[56]

If one accepts this definition, *the criterion of the Common good presents a fundamental principle of moral judgement of the organisation of a society, including the global system.*[57]

The specific contribution that the company can today bring to the global Common Good begins to take shape in the thinking and the work that calls into question our development model.

The United Nations suggests the concept of **sustainable development**.

This new model offers a true vision of the future aiming to place economic activity within the context of a global common good. Its

---

[55] See the *Compendium* of the social doctrine of the Catholic Church.

[56] Berten, I., 2009, *op. cit.*

[57] *Ibid.*

definition is well known. It is that of the Brundtland Report[58]: *Sustainable development is development that addresses the needs of the present without compromising the ability of future generations to answer their own.*

The Church goes further. For Paul VI, real development must be *integral*, that is to say *promoting each and every man.*[59]

The vision of the Church gives the development its true anthropological and theological dimension: a Creator associating man with his creation, fraternity, justice and the dignity of each person, the universal destination of earthly goods.

This view of development emphasises *the solidarity* that must be considered as a *social principle authorising institutions, by virtue of which "structures of sin" that dominate the relationship between individuals and peoples must be exceeded and transformed into "structures of solidarity", through the appropriate development or change in laws, of market rules or the creation of institutions.*[60]

It is a perspective that opens up channels of co-operation between different people and that could give hope to those who see no other option than violence.

What perspective and what inspiration! What a pity that so many Christian leaders commit themselves to it so timidly! Should they not demonstrate more of the "political" role that the company must play in order to contribute to the concrete implementation of this new development model? Should they not further explain this doctrine to give it the economic specificity that would further guide the action and the strategies of the company?

Should it not also be compared to other attempts made in this field in order to facilitate the collaborative processes, to enrich debate and accelerate the emergence of a global Common Good?

One may think, for example, of the Universal Declaration of Human Rights, of the Global Compact Principles, to the Millennium Development Goals...

---

[58] ONU, *Notre avenir à tous (Our common future)*, Les éditions du fleuve, Montréal, 1989.

[59] *Populorum Progressio*, nn. 2, 13.

[60] *Compendium, op. cit.*, 193.

Increased political participation

The social doctrine of the Church tells us that *all conscience is challenged and invited to interact with every other conscience in freedom, in full co-responsibility with everyone, in respect of all. Indeed, man cannot evade the question of truth and meaning of social life, insofar as society is not a foreign reality to its own existence.*[61]

It also calls upon us to contribute to the emergence of global governance.

> For the government of the world economy, to stabilise economies hit by the crisis, to prevent its escalation and greater imbalances, to conduct a full and desirable disarmament, to have food safety and peace, to ensure environmental protection and to regulate fluctuating migration, it is urgent to implement a real Global Political Authority…[62]

Its perspective is one of democracy, which is the form of political organisation best suited to modern societies. It is "co-natural" to them[63]. Debate is the very condition of it and the principal means.

Jacqueline de Romilly[64] reminds us that the emergence of democracy has given to the shared **debate** an unexpected dimension.

The most original principle of this regime was to *invite thousands of citizens to openly and incessantly debate on proposals and ideas … Talking, explaining, convincing one another: this is what Athens was proud of, what the texts continue to exalt… Thus Euripides, when he celebrates democracy, by the mouth of Theseus, in The Suppliants, writes with flair: "As for freedom, it is in these words: he who wants to, he who can give wise advice to his country? Then, at its will, everyone can shine or be silent. Can you imagine a more beautiful equality?"*

The questions raised today by globalisation and the techno-sciences have major importance for our future. They do not have an obvious answer. Entrepreneurs, markets and financiers

---

[61] *Compendium of the social doctrine, op. cit.*
[62] Benedict XVI, Caritas in veritate, 2009.
[63] Ladrière, J., *op. cit.*
[64] de Romilly, J., *Pourquoi la Grèce? (Why Greece?)*, Paris, Editions de Fallois, 1992.

could not be alone in directing our economic or technological evolution even if it is their specific field of activity. Sustainable development concerns all citizens, it comes under the public domain.

To decide what kind of society we want to create together, should we not listen to those who want to "speak up"?

> The same person can all at once take care of his own business and that of the State; and when people hold different occupations, they can however judge public affairs leaving nothing to be desired...We consider the man who plays no part, not as a quiet citizen, but as a useless one; and by ourselves, we consider and reason with the issues as we should; because words are not in our eyes an obstacle to action: it is one, however, for not being informed first of all by the words before addressing the action to take.[65]

Concerning involvement in political debate, are many leaders not still often "useless citizens"?

Political involvement is in man's nature.[66] It is the noblest dimension of human activity. Giving it up, above all if one has economic power, is to cut oneself out of the community, its debates and its aspirations. It is to lock oneself in a situation without legitimacy, since it rests on the special interest guided by a simple logic of means rather than a recognised and accepted aim.

Is an approach based on debate realistic on a global level?

Given the positions of power in the world and the interests at stake, realism seems to indicate that a democratic approach in the Western sense of the term is unlikely.

Indeed, the dominant power of economic actors – private and public – will not allow itself to be challenged or limited in the name of the global Common Good that is still barely defined. Add to this the weakness of most nation states and their difficulty implementing

---

[65] Thucydide, Discours de Périclès sur les premiers morts de la guerre, in *Histoire de la guerre du Péloponnèse* trans. J. de Romilly Paris, Robert Laffont, 1990.

[66] Arendt, A., *La condition de l'homme moderne (The condition of modern man)*, trans. G. Fradier, Paris, Calmann-Lévy, 1961.

long-term strategies in a concerted way. We know that *feeling and reason do not bear heavily in the face of power realities.*[67]

Without a radical and rapid outburst of major political powers (G 20), of all economic actors and of civil society, the most likely scenario will be that of increasingly serious and increasingly frequent crises. This will lead us to delayed reactions under the pressure of ecological disasters and social violence. This is what we call adaptation by crisis.

The other way is that of anticipation based on consultation, negotiation and some major agreements between major States and implemented by actors "on the ground". This is what the United Nations have already successfully initiated in the areas of health, culture, international trade... It consists here in a form of governance in which the enlightened business leaders are beginning to participate.

> The concept of governance, to the image of the regulation of complex networks of all kinds (the issue of the Internet is currently open), refers in an essentially vague way to all regulatory mechanisms in place in human systems (companies and other organisations, States, collectives of States...) that are not built around a central decisive unit, but that bring into play ad hoc co-ordination arrangements, and to a variable contingent in both time and space. Like an organisational principle, governance opposes the notion of hierarchy. One may link the idea of subsidiarity to it.[68]

This is where the political involvement of business leaders finds meaning.

The point of this approach is to design the transformation of our development model as *a process* and not as a plan fixed in advance. The angle of attack of this is not to propose a menu of rules and guidelines but to implement a complex process bringing different types of actors into play. Who says complex and co-ordinated process

---

[67] De Gaulle, Ch., *Le fil de l'épée (The edge of the sword)*, Paris, Librairie générale française, 1962.

[68] Montbrial de, T., *Le Monde au tournant du siècle (The World at the turn of the century)*, Ramsès, Paris, 2000, Dunod, 2000. See also Collomb, B. and Drancourt, M., *Plaidoyer pour l'Entreprise*, François Bourin Editeur, 2010.

reveals uncertainty in outcome and time. This perspective is therefore that of a debate on the necessary global change, including *self-regulatory mechanisms as well as restrictive guidelines at the political level*. It is through social and societal innovations, broad consultations, and new forms of negotiation that, gradually, a model of sustainable development could be put in place. It is through a true collective action-research on a global scale that this model will find the means to serve a Common Good that has become worldwide.

Many companies are beginning to move in this direction but, despite their power and their weight, alone, they will not succeed in transforming our development model. A collective and global effort is necessary. Change must take place across the three complementary levels of politics, the economy and civil society.

In this regard, the Dom Cabral Foundation and AccountAbility have developed a useful conceptual model.[69] It offers the greatest possible convergence of the initiatives of three major groups of players:

- *The political leaders (Policy Drivers)*, notably responsible for the ratification and the application of treaties on the environment, for the respect of human rights and, particularly those of workers, for poverty and mechanisms of redistribution, competition rules … Among the key players at this level are intergovernmental agencies, particularly those of the United Nations;
- *The economic leaders*, notably responsible for directing strategies and the ethical behaviour of companies, for equal pay for comparable jobs, for the stringency of accounts and controls, for staff training,… Here, the key players are clearly the multinational companies and the large industrial federations.
- *The leaders of civil society (Social Enablers)*, notably responsible for setting consumer trends, resisting corruption, for NGO initiatives, the watchful eye of the press, a denunciation of violations of clean air and water,… In this regard, the role of

---

[69] Boechat et al., *The Responsible Competitiveness Index*, in The State of Responsible Competitiveness 2007, AccountAbility and Fundaçao Dom Cabral.

NGOs continues to grow deservedly seeing as they represent a growing part of our collective consciousness.

One must emphasise the essential interdependence of the initiatives and commitments. Only the convergence of the actions will lead the way to a universal Common Good and replace our economic system in the ethical and political perspective that will give it its true purpose.

In this respect, do Christian leaders adequately unite their voices with those of other international initiatives that are trying to change our development model?

One can cite, for example, United Nations Global Compact (UNGC), The World Business Council for Sustainable Development, the Global Responsible Leadership Initiative (GRLI), CSR Europe...

Are we sufficiently active in putting these initiatives into place and in the intellectual and spiritual direction of their work?

Faced with the challenges of the 21st century, it is necessary that business leaders involve themselves in societal debates and do not let unidimensional thinking continue to contaminate the planet. To become globally responsible, they should contribute to the correction of the excessive decoupling of the economy from politics and ethics.

If the company wishes to regain its civic dimension, it must develop in it a political culture in the fullest sense of the term, it must insert its action in the life of the city and participate in debates about the Common Good and the direction of our future. Beyond mere lobbying, business leaders and executives should enter into a permanent dialogue with civil society and the public authorities to contribute to the search for a Common Good on a worldwide scale as well as the emergence of global governance. This is a normal consequence of the broadening of purposes and the adoption of an ethic of foresight.

Without such progress, the leaders and executives risk remaining locked in their instrumental logic and resembling those of the old school of thought who were incapable of reforming it.

> Several were, however, very skilful in their professions; they completely possessed all of the details of the administration...; but as to the great science of government, that learns to understand the general movement of society, to judge what goes on in the minds of the masses and

to anticipate what will result from it, they were all so new that the people themselves...

Their mind was thus stopped at the point of view where that of their fathers had been placed...

There, where assemblies conserve for nothing to change their ancient constitution, they halt the progress of civilisation rather than helping it. One might say that they are foreign and impenetrable to the new spirit of the times.[70]

A big European boss told me recently: "We are used to dialogue with trade unions or governments and we find it useful. As for NGOs, I cannot stand them: they are not legitimate, they are aggressive, they reject any discussion". Indeed some NGOs do not aid mutual understanding, but this is in the process of changing. Moreover, the converse is often true: unidimensional thinking and the traditional employer culture support neither communication, listening, nor debate over the direction of the system or the purpose of the company.

However, the most enlightened leaders understand that a cultural development in the area of politics will happen through the acceptance of an open debate with those who question our development model. The agreement, often cited, between Lafarge and the World Wildlife Fund to reduce greenhouse gas emissions, is exemplary in this regard.

If the company wishes to reintegrate its action for economic progress in the broader set of ethics and politics, the first requirement is to listen to society and to talk more about it.

Is there not a danger that such a development replaces action with endless discussions?

The traditional leaders think and say so. They believe that the debates and the "chit-chat" are useless, if not curbing their actions, hindering their dynamism, diminishing their creativity. We must resist this scepticism. In an uncertain, complex and dangerous world, debate is better than lobbying. In the current ethical and political vacuum, issues of purpose, value and power must be raised, discussed and guided towards solutions that respond to the challenges of the future rather than being left to the apathy of unidimensional

---

[70] Tocqueville, A. de, *L'ancien régime et la révolution (The former regime and the revolution)*, Gallimard, 1952.

thought. In a democratic perspective, the return of politics, that's it! And the company will only be truly accountable to the extent that it will actively engage in dialogue *on the fundamentals.*

The procedural approach opens up bright prospects in this area.

Developed by the philosopher Jürgen Habermas,[71] it aims to organise in a more systematic manner the methods and forms of consultation.

In a pluralistic world like ours, the relevance and credibility of a normative system (one rule, one decision...) does not only lie in its conformity to any ideal-type (a system of predetermined values for example) but in the manner in which this rule or this decision has been made. Such an approach is aimed at all concerned persons (*stakeholders*) who have been able to agree on the debate process before beginning the discussion of the content.

This pathway would appear to be like a practicable trail for the renewal and deepening of democracy[72] and to prevent the system from overwhelming the actors.

The return of a political culture in the company is necessitated by the fact that it is not an island, that we are part of a democracy and that the evolution of our development model must be based on the support of citizens. A broader consultation could contribute to this mightily.

> Because we received the power to mutually persuade each other and to clarify for ourselves the subject of our decisions, not only did we get rid of primitive life, but we were reunited to build towns; we established laws; we discovered the arts; and in almost all of our inventions, it is words that have enabled us to successfully complete them...[73]

Speech and debate are really at the origin of civilisation and the overall progress of society.

This does not negate the need to regulate global economic games.

---

[71] Habermas, J., *Théorie de l'agir communicationnel (Theory of communicative action),* Paris, Fayard, 1987; and *De l'éthique de la discussion (The ethics of the discussion),* Paris, Editions du Cerf, 1992.

[72] Cobbaut, R. and Lenoble, J., *Corporate Governance, an Institutionalist Approach,* Kluwer Law International, The Hague, 2003.

[73] Isocrate, *Sur l'échange (On the exchange),* in J. de Romilly, *op. cit.*

Overall rules are necessary and urgent to correct major malfunctions and to promote the emergence of a more sustainable and fairer development model.

> Between the strong and the weak, between the rich and the poor, it is the law that liberates and liberty that oppresses. *(Lacordaire)*

Within the Judeo-Christian tradition, the law is presented as the very mark of wisdom and civilisation. When it is well made, the law is a blessing.

It ensures fairness and harmony, it helps one follow the pathways of a civilised life, it restricts the temptations for dehumanisation by domination and exclusion.

> [The law] will show your wisdom and understanding to the nations, who will hear about all these decrees and say, "Surely this great nation is a wise and understanding people." *(Deuteronomy 4:6)*

> The Law, *more desirable than gold,*
> *than a mass of fine gold,*
> *sweeter than honey*
> *running freely. (Psalm: 19)*

THE "DAY TO DAY", CONCRETE COMMON GOOD[74]

There is a new and interesting concept allowing us to better understand our concrete and specific responsibility in the achievement of the Common Good.

Concrete Common Goods are constituted by the quality of relationships at different levels of existence: family, work, politics, education, leisure, etc... *They constitute the backdrop of human existence: the atmosphere or the ambience that produce the social situations of coexistence and that mingle with the feeling of existing (or of not existing) experienced by everyone.* They form *the relational basis that gives meaning* and in the context of which working life, leisure or civic life are practised. Concrete Common Goods directly support the feeling of existence of

---

[74] This section draws directly on Flahault, F., *op. cit.*

the people who live by them. They therefore constitute an end in themselves.

... if politics have begun to consider the planet as a human habitat, they have still not realised at what point social life also constitutes itself the vital habitat of the human being.

Current rationalism and instrumental logic often prevent modern man from fitting into a habitat that is truly human, that creates *this fundamental experience: the feeling of existing alongside others in the same world. The "economicity" that has gripped minds placed them in the incapacity to think, what is a society? ...*

It is there that business leaders have an important responsibility: that of creating a workplace that is entirely human.

Awareness of the domestic situation of workers is also an important aspect if we want to preserve this central value of our civilisation, this being the family.

Many leaders are working to achieve these "Concrete Common Goods". Are they enough? Should we not study and further disseminate their initiatives and their innovations?

The example of the company Ouimet, already mentioned, is very convincing and shows that this may be compatible with strong economic performance.[75]

This experience is all the more impressive as it is based on a modern anthropology and takes account of the most fundamental human aspirations, including spiritual aspirations.

It is this kind of achievement that can make a decisive contribution to the development of Concrete Common Goods and to the rejuvenation of the thinking of business leaders.

According to the foregoing considerations, the 21st Century company that would like to act responsibly should find a new balance between the three major dimensions of its activities:

- *Entrepreneurship*: economic and technical **creation**,
- *Leadership*: sense giving, sense making and bearer of humane **values**,
- *Statesmanship*: civic participation in the **common good**.

---

[75] Ouimet, R., *op. cit.*

Committing itself in this way is to realise a change in **the very culture of the company.**

Indeed, defining its *raison d'être* in terms of progress rather than profit alone, putting ethics at the heart of strategic decisions and behaviour, opening up to debates on a global Common Good and trying to implement it in its specific domain, all this suggests a renewed vision of the company.

The advantage of a clear vision is to enable those who share it to be pulled forward by the future rather than passively pushed by the past. Such a vision will allow leaders and executives to bring about a more sustainable development model and to give their economic and technical power a legitimacy that is required today for it to be exerted usefully.

Faced with the urgency of the challenges that confront us, dare we, quickly enough, design and implement this new business and development model?

Will Christian leaders, enlightened by their values and led by their faith, play a significant role in this, measuring up to the doctrine and a revelation that invites them to engage in the human adventure via creation, fraternity and solidarity and to transform it in the story of salvation? That is the question that this essay is attempting to ask.

CHAPTER 3

NEW HEARTS

I will give you a new heart and put a new spirit in you,[1] says the Lord:
I will create new heavens and a new earth [where justice will reign].[2]

The transformation of our economic system will only be sustainable if the men and women who lead it are transformed themselves. Changes in structures will not happen "by order". They will only come to life if they are driven from within by people of good will. This is where Christians can play a major role. Are we not called to be the *salt of the earth* and *light on the mountain*?

Saint Paul constantly invites us to *become new human beings, created holy and fair, in the likeness of God.*[3]

The testimonies of Christian leaders who are trying to unify their professional lives and their religious lives are all headed in the same direction: the conscious commitment in their own humanisation and in a process of deepening their freedom and their choices;

- an ethical will and the refusal to be locked into a system or a unidimensional thought;
- a feeling of humility and fragility before the complexity of their profession; the choice of faith and of a real-life faith; the attachment to Christ and an intense spiritual life thanks to prayer, sacrament, readings, retreats and interviews; attention for the other and a great capacity for listening. All this often made wise people, but without superiority, welcoming and often peaceful.

---

[1] Ezekiel 36:26.
[2] Isaiah 65:17.
[3] Eph. 3:24.

These stories are touching, they ring true, they pass on an existential knowledge as convincing as living convictions.[4]

Should the movements of Christian leaders not study and disseminate them more?

BECOMING HUMAN

> The Lord said to Abram, leave your country, your people and your fathrr's household and go to the land I will show you...
> So Abram left as the Lord had told him. *(Genesis 12:1–4)*

> Get up, go away!
> For this is not your resting place... *(Micah 2:10)*

> A man is not born a man, but becomes one. *(Erasmus)*

> In God's plan, every man is expected to grow because all of life is a vocation.[5]

> *Every man is a sacred story. (Liturgical song)*

Becoming human is a journey, a quest, an inner creation.

It is the gradual construction of a conscience, autonomy, responsible freedom. Psychology shows that it is a "becoming", an emergence, of a work on oneself.

> The meaning of human life is that of a journey that will lead to an accomplishment...
> Man is given to himself, not like a completed being who would only let himself live, but as a being who is to do, who is gradually called upon to give himself his true form...

> Man in his autonomy and his responsibility is the bearer of a destiny

---

[4] There are a certain number of them. I would like to cite two of them that I find particularly convincing: that of Robert Ouimet, *Tout vous a été confié (All has been entrusted to you)*, *(op. cit.)* and that of Olivier Lecerf, *Au risque de gagner (At the risk of winning)*, Paris, Editions de Fallois, 1991.

[5] *Caritas in veritate*, 16.

that is both singular and collective, shaper of his own history, open to an infinite horizon of meaning.[6]

We are therefore temporal beings with a destiny to achieve. While in French 'destin' (fate) and 'destinée' (destiny) are synonyms, they do not come from the same place in theology where fate is undergone and contains in itself a certain fatality while destiny is for Mankind to conquer. Indeed, by definition, we are developing beings, never completed.[7]

The Humanists of the Renaissance do not say otherwise.

I have given you neither a determined place, nor a face of your own, nor any particular gift, O Adam, so that your place, your face and your gifts, you may will, conquer and possess by yourself. *(Pic de la Mirandole)*

And Sartre:

Without equipment, without tools, I set all of me to work in order to save all of me. If I relegate impossible Salvation to the prop-room, what remains? A whole man, composed of all men and as good as all of them and no better than any.[8]

DARING TO BE FRAGILE

... I am a frail man, too weak to understand the precepts and the laws. *(Wisdom 9, 2)*

Becoming human is to recognise oneself as creator, but also as fragile and bound.[9] It is often difficult for a Promethean leader.

Modern anthropology reminds us of our fundamental duality, the existential tension that we are forced to assume: our aspirations for existence and creation co-habit with great incompletion, a gap that apparently nothing can fill. On the one hand, an unlimited desire, on

---

[6] Ladrière, J., *op. cit.*, 1985.
[7] Cochinaux, Ph., *op. cit.*
[8] Sartre, J.P., *Les mots (Words)*, Paris, Gallimard, 1964.
[9] This paragraph draws directly from Arnsperger, Ch., *op. cit.*

the other, our finitude and our limitations. We would like to exist fully and unconditionally but we are faced with certain death and faced with others, "the other", strange, different, worrying.

To exist is to live as mortals, together with other mortals.

Does civilisation not consist in the courage to *manage this double finitude in order* to create a more authentically human society, *to transform this existential tension into a creative force rather than a destructive force?*

Man is a social being, bound to others, member of a society that must help him to overcome his weaknesses and his fears and to achieve his aspirations.

This perspective emphasises the relational being compared to the isolated individual, whatever its strength or its talents. It calls on us to be creative without falling into the Promethean excesses, arrogance or the illusion of omnipotence, to recognise itself as fraternal, fragile and interdependent. The real hero is not the cosmic hero of myths or romance but that which *co-exists with others all the while being open to its own fear of finitude as well as that of others.*

> One hardly has to have lived to see or guess that a virtual label is stuck to the front of each of us: "attention, fragile".[10]

> To ignore that man has a wounded nature, inclined towards the bad leads to serious errors in the domain of education, politics, social and moral action.[11]

If it depends upon a deep work on oneself, becoming human is also a social work and it is here that courage can become collective. Since man is a relational being, he cannot fully exist without this interdependence on society that contributes to his construction and places him in a collective that influences him, supports him and enriches him. Contrary to the individual, the person is unique but linked to others. It is this relationship that makes it recognisable as human in its creations, aspirations and fragility. It is here that it can

---

[10] Grenet, X., *Cahier d'un DRH (Notebook of a DRH)*, Paris, Cerf, 2008.

[11] *Centesimus annus*, n. 36.

be aware of fraternity and essential solidarity. It is there that it can understand that existence does not reduce it to rationality alone nor to the world of "things" or knowledge. It is also here that it can feel the vanity of arrogant behaviour or excessive individualism.

In situations of power, there is strong temptation to exaggerate, to believe oneself to be above ordinary people or to prioritise relationships with "things" more than with human beings.

As entrepreneurs, shall we allow ourselves to be tempted by the Promethean excesses and pride, by *arrogance, boldness, challenges, the exaltation of oneself, appetite for power, cynicism, lack of scruples*, or shall we bear in mind our fragility, a fraternity to share in, compassion, listening to others, guided by the values of the Gospel?

For the Christian, courage is a cardinal virtue, but it differs from old courage and Nietzschean harshness.[12]

It is not sought primarily for personal success, prestige or "glory" but for the coming of the Kingdom, a world of justice, peace and love.

Its source lies not solely in the will or stoicism of a near superhuman hero, but in a spirituality that relies on the Spirit promised by Christ, spirit of love, wisdom and strength. Rooted in a human nature that knows fragility and hurt, courage then becomes a continuous, humble, patient and concrete existential effort.

It is also seen in terms of initiative and creativity, as "the courage to begin" (Saint Augustine), the courage to undertake.

Once again, man has been created creator!

Here it consists in the courage to undertake and situate his "company" within the perspective of a Common Good that becomes global. It consists in the political courage to try to answer the question of knowing what world we want to build and to commit ourselves to its construction.

It also consists in having the courage to question the model that one leads whatever its advantages, its power or its promises.

With a heart of poverty we must have the courage to address the problems of our times and to exercise our creativity:

---

[12] Voir Berns, et al. *op. cit.*

...unless you change and become like little children, you will never enter the kingdom of heaven.[13]

CHOOSING THE SPIRIT

When Christian leaders testify to their faith, they talk not only of grace but also of a choice and a commitment constantly renewed. This choice of faith, they most often made in full awareness of the horrible tragedies of human history, notably Auschwitz, and also of scientific advances and the new discoveries touching the universe, life and the depths of our psychology. Their commitment is part of a coherent vision of destiny where *Reason and Faith mutually help each other because it is only together that they will save man.*[14]

In considering the evolution of the universe (the arrow of time), one cannot help but question this movement, this momentum, which drives matter to life and life to man, being capable of freedom, creativity, love and wonderment

This somewhat gifted being has not ceased to undertake magnificent adventures that have contributed to humanize the earth and create civilisations: language, awareness and discernment between the best and the worst, religious questioning, law and justice, democracy, intellectual and artistic creations, the extraordinary journey of science, technical innovations, exchange and economic development, the sake of our neighbour, charitable works, social welfare...

Is there not here as a guide, a pathway, a positive drift towards what might be called the humanisation of the world.

But we also know that this being, capable of civilisation, is also capable of the contrary.

Next to this momentum of freedom, Mankind has experienced dictatorship, tyranny, oppression and barbarity. Even if intellectual creativity discovers the world and makes more sense of it, knowledge has often been used for dangerous or harmful purposes.

---

[13] Matthieu 18:5.
[14] *Caritas in veritate*, 74.

Even if there is love, history is also marred with hatred, violence and cruelty.

We stand before the enigma of a human being, capable of the highest and the lowest acts:

- Greatness and misery of man *(Pascal)*
- Man mixes light and darkness *(Confucius)*

However, as Menander said, man is pleasant, when he is man!

Man ... *is an angel, is an animal, is nothingness, is a miracle, is the centre, is a world, is a God, is nothingness surrounded by God, capable of God, filled with God if he wants it. (Bérulle)*[15]

All of civilisation has been aware of it.

The question then appears to be: is the evolution that leads to man and all of his creations due to chance or does it have a meaning?

A question as old as the world.

> We came into being by chance and afterwards shall be as though we had never been... All those things have passed like a shadow... *(Wisdom, 2:2 and 5:9)*

Is life but *a walking shadow, a poor player that struts and frets his hour upon the stage, and then is heard no more? Is it a tale told by an idiot, full of sound and fury, signifying nothing? (Shakespeare)*

Or are we actually destined to participate in and live out a human adventure to which we could give meaning?

Religions and great spiritual messages suggest a meaning and offer us a choice.

There would be like a breath, a Spirit that would inspire, raise, and invite man to become more human.

If one takes the trouble to distinguish the spiritual message of the religions from the contingencies of their history – they were often recovered for political ends or reduced to issues of power or interests – one must admit that wherever this Spirit has blown, the level was raised, and humanisation progressed.

---

[15] Bérulle, P.de, 1575–1629, cited by Gesché, 1993.

Would God not be this Spirit that invites man to become more humane and to develop the world in the sense of freedom, love and peace?

Would he not be this call to Life, this impetus for love, this light that illuminates the road and invites us, despite the limits of suffering and death, to become and remain alive by adhering to the only never-ending life: that of everlasting love?

A transcendence that would force no one, that would satisfy itself by inviting, offering, by inspiring, and that would be gentle.

The God of the Bible is not in the sound of thunder, nor in the flash of lightening nor in the roar of the storm. He is in the light breeze . . .

It is adherence to this momentum of humanisation and love that characterises the choices of the most committed Christians.

FOLLOWING CHRIST
I am the way, the truth and the life.

The God of the Gospel has taken the humblest and most deprived form: that of the crucified.

By assuming our fragile nature, Christ teaches us that there is true salvation in living by his message and enjoining us to the force of the Spirit and the love of the Father.

By inviting us to follow him, Jesus offers us an existential truth. It is not contrary to the truth of science but it exceeds it and gives it depth where this is lacking. It addresses the real human problems and commits us to action, but with humility and respect for everyone. There is no acceptable triumphalism for a God of tenderness and love. The image of a loving Father is incompatible with domination, violence, intolerance or the refusal of the other.

> Love is an extraordinary force that pushes people to commit with courage and generosity in the area of justice and peace. It is a force that originates in God, Love and Absolute Truth.[16]

> Rather than lock oneself into an ethic of action, it is better to turn towards an ethic of being. This does not concern itself primarily with actions but rather the person who poses them. The ethics of being seeks

---

[16] *Caritas in veritate*, 1.

to provide an answer to the question of knowing: 'Who do I want to become?'. Having found it, there will result a set of actions that should be taken in order to allow the person to become what it wants to be.[17]

Christians who really want to follow Christ know that prayer and spirituality will help them to do so and will strengthen their commitment and their efforts to humanise the Creation.

> I am the vine, you are the branches ... No branch can bear fruit by itself; it must remain in the vine.[18]

> Our life revolves around an empty centre that can only be filled by the Holy Spirit.[19]

> In the economic and financial professions, there are lots of people for whom Jesus Christ is a true personal reference in their faith. There is not incompatibility between finance and belonging to Christianity.[20]

Many testimonies on prayer come from these leaders.

For Robert Ouimet, already cited, it involves *basing the daily lives of every organisation on certain spiritual values*[21] and on a true spirituality. It evokes:

> the strength, the irreplaceable character, the primacy of inner silence, that silence which leads to prayer...
> I discovered that work could become a silent prayer: ora et labora...
> Today, I feel more fragile than ever as man faced with love, facing the ability to love. But now I live all the while praying, that is to say in closeness with Christ...

Charles de Liedekerke insists on the importance of prayer and spirituality to enlighten and animate the three spheres of

---

[17] Cochinaux, Ph., *op. cit.*

[18] John 15:4–5.

[19] Radcliff, Th., at the general congress of Benedictines, 2007.

[20] Herr, E., *Et vous, qui dites-vous que je suis ? (And you, who would you say that I am?)* Carême 2008 à ND de Paris.

[21] Ouimet, J.-R., *op. cit.*

responsibility of the leader: his person, his company, his social surroundings.[22]

Olivier Lecerf declares:

> My system of values has been inspired by the discovery of the Gospel which may have been the greatest event of my life. From that moment on, I understood that I belonged as everyone does to the clan of the "weak and sinners"...
>
> Every individual must make daily choices between the necessary and the optional, the good and the bad, the desirable and the undesirable. To this "secular" meditation, of course I add prayer.[23]

Should we not more systematically gather these testimonies and reconcile them with contemporary research on spirituality and management?[24]

This would allow us to strengthen this domain and to disseminate the message across more objectively.[25]

For Christian leaders and executives, the personal reference to Jesus gives them a renewed vision of the purpose of their creative action and new directions to give to the system that they lead.

> Thomas said to him... how can we know the way? Jesus answered: I am the way and the truth and the life...[26]

> "Who do you say that I am?" These words were addressed by Jesus to his disciples, but we may consider that spiritually they still apply to us today... It is not the anxious questioning of a narcissistic character, but the invitation, in the form of a question, to engage in an Alliance with God in Jesus Christ.

---

[22] de Liedekerke, Ch., *Dirigeant chrétien (The Christian Leader)*, Rencontres N. and D. de Flue, Novembre 2006.

[23] Lecerf, O., *Au risque de gagner. Le métier de dirigeant (At the risk of winning. The profession of leader)*, Ed. de Fallois, 1991.

[24] See notably, del Marmol, G., *Tomber plus haut (Falling higher)*, Paris, Alphée, 2009. Zohar, D., and Marshall, I., *Spiritual Capital*, London, Bloomsbury, 2004.

[25] See notably Audoyer, J.P., *op. cit.*

[26] John 14:5–6.

From a systemic point of view, this implies that the financial system is integral in the story of salvation with God... This is possible insomuch as financial globalisation answers the ethical and political inquiry of opening up to the Common Good notably in terms of crises and distribution of profits... In other words, the initial question of Jesus "who do you say that I am?" is thus reformulated: "what will become of the poor and the weak in the world financial system?"[27]

You send forth your Spirit... and you renew the face of the earth *(Psalm 103)*

But the fruit of the Spirit is love, joy, peace, patience, kindness, goodness, faithfulness, gentleness and self-control. *(Paul, Galatians 5:22)*

It is in Christ that all shall live again. *(Paul, Cor. 15:25)*

CREATING THE ENCOUNTER

The heart has almost disappeared from our "systems".

Balzac already spoke of the *wheels of polished steel of modern society.*

O princes with heart of iron! said Erasmus

Let us be wary of the *harshness that all*[28] *form of power produces, the glaciation of the soul.*

Let us defy the cynical adage of those that dominate and repeat with a grin:

One leads men with the head, one does not play chess with a kind heart *(Chamfort)*

Never consider men as pawns, even if one is a financier!

There is so little love in the world, hearts are so cold, so frozen, even in those who are right, the only ones who could help others. One must have a strong mind and a kind heart. Not counting listless minds of terse heart, the world is nearly only made up of harsh minds with terse heart and gentle hearts with listless mind.[29]

---

[27] Herr, E., *op. cit.*

[28] Zweig, S., *op. cit.*

[29] Maritain, J., *Réponse à Jean Cocteau, in Œuvres complètes de Jacques et Raïssa Maritain (Response to Jean Cocteau in the Complete works of Jacques and Raïssa Maritan)*, Les Editions Saint Paul, Paris, 1985. This pearl of wisdom was given to me by Nicolas Buttet.

If man is a relational being, the quality and depth of these relations are never indifferent. Must we not often dare to transform the relationship into encounter?[30]

The meeting commits the heart. It is the personalised relationship, on an equal and reciprocal footing, without mediation of money or power. It is the place of mutual acceptance, listening, watching, the place where one can be "called by his name", accepting its fragility, recognising the other, making it exist, helping it to stand up. It is the place of the communion, the place where one can watch the other with eyes of love.

Here it consists in finding words, sharing.

Communicating means: pooling something; conversing: turning towards each other; dialoguing: daring to speak about meaning.

For certain leaders, the assessment interview, done humanely, could be a true meeting opportunity. At the heart of every meeting is our ability to listen.

> Listening is an available time and space, the offering of a place and a peaceful moment, of tranquillity, of less stress ... Listening is the virtue of the poor within each of us. It requires neither diplomas nor titles, and this is why it is probably too infrequently practised by the powerful.[31]

> I will give you a new heart
> and put a new spirit in you;
> I will remove from you your heart of stone
> and give you a heart of flesh.
> (Ezekiel 36:26)

SEARCHING FOR WISDOM

> Since you have asked ... for discernment in administering justice ... I will give you a wise and discerning heart. (Kings 3:10)

> I entreated and the spirit of Wisdom came to me.
> I esteemed her more than sceptres and thrones.

---

[30] For the whole passage, see Vanier, J., op. cit.

[31] Grenet, X., op. cit.

Compared with her, I held riches as nothing...
I loved her more than health or beauty,
preferred her to the light,
since her radiance never sleeps. *(Wisdom 7, 7:10)*

Faced with folly and barbarity, hasten the return of wisdom and heart!

Is wisdom anything other than intelligence coined by the soul and the heart?

Wisdom is the breath of God's power ... it is strength and gentleness.

Let us not enter the pitfalls of rationalism or scientism.

Everyone knows the methodological limitations of science.

It is only one of the methods of knowledge available to us. It only delivers us the part of reality that it discovers by its methods.[32] It says nothing about the uniqueness of people, nothing about sense or purpose, nothing serious about moral suffering, evil or destiny. In short, it does not really talk about man.

These existential questions are outside its domain. They are however at the heart of our lives and of a responsible construction of the future.

Bernard d'Espagnat, theoretical physicist, questions the ultimate veracity of this scientific approach:

> I understand, not its veracity as a convenient model, a useful guide for action, etc. – evident and thus undeniable veracity – but its "ontological" truth,... excluding that there is nothing deeper.

We know the truth not only by reason but also by the heart *(Pascal)*

The Spirit of truth will guide you towards the whole truth *(John 15:13)*

Should we not go further and dare prophetic charisma? If all of society needs stability, it also requires evolutionary forces. It consists in having the courage to oppose institutions and systems when they slip. The prophetic role is the most dynamic form of wisdom. It is to

---

[32] d'Espagnat, B., *Une réouverture des chemins du sens (A reopening of meaningful ways)*, in Staune, J., *Sciences et quête de sens (Science and the quest for meaning)*, PUF, 2005.

question the direction of our society and to see the consequences of its excesses and its disfunctions. The prophets *tell the news of God in the present and for the present, both as good news and as a challenge to everything that is demonstrated as contrary to God's will* ... The prophets are *symbols of humanity* ... *they are an expression of the historical condition of our humanity and of the values that transcend particular historic circumstances.*[33]

If one is Christian, why would one not want to transform our economic system and correct its defects? Once again, this is not to destroy it but to improve it, to amend it, to direct it more towards the Common Good and the responsibilisation of all its actors.

> Indeed, were anyone perfect among the sons of men,
> if he lacked the Wisdom that comes from you,
> he would still count for nothing.
> With you is Wisdom,
> she who knows your works ...
> she who was present [when you made the world] ...
> Send her out that she may be with me and may labour with me
> she will guide me prudently in my actions ... *(Wisdom 9:1–12)*

ENGAGING IN HOPE

The Twentieth Century was a century of violence, destruction and suffering: two world wars, the holocaust, other genocides, concentration camps, tyrannies, civil wars, ethnic cleansing, Hiroshima ...

It speaks sadly of all human history, this history "full of noise and fury."

It probably tells of the future: destruction of the planet, dissemination of weapons of mass destruction, terrorism, pandemic, poverty, economic violence ...

We can no longer speak of God as if Auschwitz never happened[34]

Can we still believe in the humanisation of creation and the rising of the Spirit?

---

[33] Berten, I., *op. cit.*

[34] Hans Jonas, *Le concept de Dieu après Auschwitz (The concept of God after Auschwitz)*, trans. Ph. Ivernel, Paris, Rivages poche, 1994.

This is **the** fundamental question in the domain that we are discussing: the scandal[35] of evil that makes so many people stumble in their quest for God.

How can a creator God, infinitely good and "almighty" allow these horrors?

Why the death of innocent people, the suffering of children, the wickedness of men?

I find that there are few convincing responses to this question.

Pascalian entertainment is not one of them.

> Men not having been able to heal death, misery and ignorance, they have decided to make themselves happy and not to think.

This is not very serious.

But what a temptation for a society imbued with consumerism, zapping (channel hopping) and short termism.

> Let us laugh at everything, for fear of being forced to cry about it (Beaumarchais at the end of the Old regime).

Blissful optimism, that of Pangloss or of unidimensional thinking, consists in believing that, if everything is still not for the best in the best of worlds, everything will inevitably improve thanks to the dynamism of the system: scientific progress, capitalist globalisation, international trade...

Fukuyama dares to announce the end of History thanks to the alliance of democracy and capitalism.

In an even more flat way, a large company proclaims its faith in cooked meats: "Who will bring the world together if McDonalds does not do it?"

It is the nature of all unidimensional thinking to blissfully believe that the effectiveness of a logic of means can do without values or purpose.

There is also reason, the development of knowledge and experimental research. Science has developed increasingly precise research

---

[35] Scandal signifies the stone on the pathway, that trips you up, the stumbling block.

methods. They explore life and matter, they discover secrets within them and their results are dazzling. For all that, do they achieve the Truth and does their work shed light on our dilemmas, on the issue of evil and that of our destiny?

Do their methods even allow them to tackle them? What serious words do they offer about moral suffering, anguish, love, art, death...? Their limits show us that there are other knowledge pathways than those that they use. By painting Guernica, does Picasso not talk better of violence and barbarity? Do the last Beethoven quartets not better contemplate death than biology or philosophy? Reason alone does not seem capable of offering an answer to the scandal of evil. For our intellect, it remains a mystery.

Commitment and hope remain. Political commitment is obviously vital for the establishment of the Common Good, for the creation of *a good life, with and for others, within the framework of fair institutions.*[36] It is no mere coincidence that Hannah Arendt considers political action to be man's noblest function. Ethical commitment, we have seen, can deeply transform our behaviour and *begins with the first cry of human suffering.*[37] It is through commitment that the responses to evil are most convincing.

That of Christ is radical: never to compromise with evil and, wherever it shows itself, to combat it and help man by trying to alleviate and share their suffering, by forgetting about oneself until sacrifice: in his case, until the supreme sacrifice.

It is not by the reason only that evil can be fought, it is also by love.

By contemplating Auschwitz, Hans Jonas suggests to us the idea that the "almightiness" of God can only exert itself in history through the women and men who embody his example of love.

It is by adhering to and living by the message of Christ, by committing oneself to the very life of Christ, that Christians will, with others, fight off evil and let the good prevail.

In the cohort of those who demonstrate a credible commitment against evil, there are all those who, through their life, touch us

---

[36] Ricœur, *La Promesse et la règle (The Promise and the rule)*, Paris, Michalon, Collect. 'Le Bien Commun, 1996.
[37] Fourez, *op. cit.*

deeply within ourselves, like, for example, Mother Theresa, Gandhi, Martin Luther King, Sister Emmanuelle, Don Helder Camara, those of ATD Fourth World, MSF and so many others.

Those there do not make scholarly discourses, they act and they bear witness; they do not talk *about* suffering but *from* it, which is a completely different language.

That the title of a book written on one of the poorest cities in the world is "The City of Joy" speaks that language to us here.

At the heart of evil there are people who fight it and whose bright smile speaks of life, love and probably eternity.

Transfigured human beings.

They make me believe that evil will not have the last word.

For Christians, hope is a "cardinal" virtue. It is of another depth than optimism. Optimism falls within the temperament or the Coué method. In this regard, Valéry cruelly said: *the optimist and the pessimist are two fools to be sent back to back. Only hope counts.*

Hope finds its source in the soul and leads to a free commitment in the creation of a better world.

It is based on the vision of a possible and progressive humanisation of the creation and on the values that can drive it. It is not at all passive, however. According to the wise words of Saint Ignatius of Loyola, it applies *to do everything as if it all depended on us and to wait for everything as it all depended on God.* It then relies on a belief in transcendence that gives meaning to life.

> Belief is not knowledge but hope. Belief is not to know but to imagine. Belief is not to end the mystery but to inhabit the mystery.[38]
>
> Now faith is the substance of things hoped for, the evidence of things not seen. *(Paul, Heb. 11:1)*
>
> God who supplies seed to the sower will both give you bread to eat and will multiply your seed and increase the growth of the fruits of your justice.[39]
>
> Following on from his finitude, reason fails to give satisfactory "reasons" to the greatest problems in human history, because there is a

---

[38] Schmitt, E.E., *J'aime cette foi fragile (I like this fragile faith)*, Panorama, August/September, 2006.
[39] Paul, Cor. 9:10.

limit to the intelligibility. It is not surprising, according to Jean Ladrière that few philosophers try to scrutinise the worrying nature of evil, or indeed that of death, or yet of suffering. Confronted with these mysteries, Mankind is in dire need of hope.[40]

A "hopeful" faith that is formulated over time...and expresses itself in the belief of *Dom Helder Camara*:

> I believe in God
> who is the Father of all men
> and who has entrusted the Earth.
> I believe in Jesus Christ who came
> to guide and to heal us,
> to deliver and teach us
> the peace of God with Mankind.
> I believe in the Spirit of God that is at work
> in every man of good will.
> I believe that man will live
> the life of God for ever more.
> I do not believe in the right of the strongest,
> in the language of weapons,
> in the power of the powerful.
> I believe in the rights of man,
> in the open hand, in the power of non violence.
> I do not believe in race or wealth,
> In privileges, in an established order.
> I believe that the whole world is my home
> I believe that the law is one, here and there,
> And that I am not free
> As long as a single man is a slave.
> I do not believe that war and hunger
> are inevitable and peace inaccessible.
> I believe in modest action,
> in love and peace on Earth.
> I do not believe that any affliction is in vain.
> I do not believe that the dream of man
> remains a dream and that death is the end.

---

[40] Mandy, P., *Jean Ladrière, un philosophe de l'espérance (Jean Ladrière, a philosopher of hope)*, Esprit, October 2008.

But I dare to believe, always and in spite of everything,
in the new man.
I dare to believe in the dream of God himself:
A new heaven, a new Earth
where righteousness dwells.

ABOUT THE AUTHOR

Philippe de Woot is Emeritus Professor at Louvain Catholic University in Belgium, where he taught Business Policy, Strategic Management and Business Ethics. He has led multidisciplinary research in these fields and is still actively committed to the research and promotion of Corporate Social Responsibility. He is the author of many books and articles on these subjects. He is a former Dean of Louvain School of Management and has taught at INSEAD as invited Professor in the Avira Program. He has been Consultant or Director of various European multi-national Corporations. He is a member of the Royal Academy of Belgium, the International Academy of Management and the European Academy for Arts and Sciences. He is Correspondent of the Institut de France.

INDEX

For Product Safety Concerns and Information please contact our EU
representative GPSR@taylorandfrancis.com Taylor & Francis Verlag GmbH,
Kaufingerstraße 24, 80331 München, Germany

Printed and bound by CPI Group (UK) Ltd, Croydon, CR0 4YY
01/05/2025
01858352-0001